Wool-on-Wool Folk Art Quilts

by
Janet Carija Brandt

That Patchwork Place®

Dedication

To all women for whom "make-thing-itis" is the happiest of afflictions.

Acknowledgments

From my mother, Virginia Carija, I learned about beautiful things. From fashion to furniture, hers has always been a classic and elegant approach. From my father, John Carija, I learned the value of good craftsmanship. From my Gramma, Mary Cizmas, I learned to hook rugs. From the Monday Night Regulars and the Puckihuddlers: Debby, Deb, Ruth, Lois, and Norma, I found help and encouragement. From editors Mary Ellen Cooper and Betsy Harris, I had my first taste of professional support and enthusiasm. From Kerry Hoffman and Laura Reinstatler at That Patchwork Place, I received inspiration, many publishing answers, and new long-distance friendships. A hearty thank you to you all. And especially, many thanks to:

Charles and Jane, and most of all, Chris.

Credits

Editor-in-Chief	Barbara Weiland
Technical Editor	Laura M. Reinstatler
Managing Editor	Greg Sharp
Copy Editor	Liz McGehee
Proofreader	Leslie Phillips
Design Director	Judy Petry
Text and Cover Designer	Kay Green
Production Assistant	Shean Bemis
Illustrator	Laurel Strand
Illustration Assistant	Lisa McKenney
Photographer	Brent Kane
Decorative Art	Barb Tourtillotte

MISSION STATEMENT

WE ARE DEDICATED TO PROVIDING QUALITY PRODUCTS THAT ENCOURAGE CREATIVITY AND PROMOTE SELF-ESTEEM IN OUR CUSTOMERS AND OUR EMPLOYEES.

WE STRIVE TO MAKE A DIFFERENCE IN THE LIVES WE TOUCH.

That Patchwork Place is an employee-owned, financially secure company.

Wool-on-Wool Folk Art Quilts
©1995 by Janet Carija Brandt

That Patchwork Place Inc.
PO Box 118
Bothell, WA 98041-0118
USA

Printed in the United States of America
00 99 98 97 96 95   6 5 4 3 2 1

Library of Congress Cataloging-in-Publication Data
Brandt, Janet Carija,
    WOW! Wool-on-wool folk art quilts / by Janet Carija Brandt.
            p.   cm.
        ISBN 1-56477-177-2
        1. Quilting—Patterns. 2. Appliqué—Patterns. 3. Wool quilts. 4 Rugs, Hooked. I. Title.
    TT835.B66 1995
    746.46–dc20   95-31192
                                                    CIP

Contents

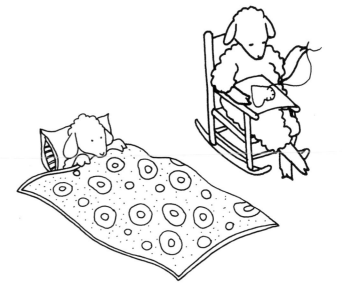

Introduction

As a teenager, I started out in fashion display and illustration, then earned a degree in architecture, only to eventually return to textiles. After hooking my first rug in 1986, I began designing my own rug-hooking patterns. In 1990 I started Carijarts, a mail-order catalog of rug hooking patterns and kits. I have written many articles for *Rug Hooking* magazine and was named among the top 200 craftsmen by *Early American Life* magazine each of the years I submitted work. Quite simply, I love to design things, whether they are built, sewn, or hooked.

I've tinkered with fabric for as long as I can remember. One day, a couple of years ago, I was hooking a rug and thinking there must be a more timely way to get the ideas out of my head and into the fabric. I had notebooks filled with ideas, shelves loaded with wool, and dye pots simmering on the stove. Why not combine the luscious textures and colors of wool as they appear in hooked rugs with the techniques of appliqué and quilting? That was the beginning of *Wool-on-Wool Folk Art Quilts*.

My designs are pure whimsy. I like to design pieces that you won't see anywhere else. After all, isn't that why we spend the time making something unique? "See, I made this!" we sometimes want to shout when we have just finished a project.

This is a book to inspire and guide you, to kindle your creative spirit. It is a chance to play with color, perhaps play with a fabric you haven't used before, to tinker anew.

MEET THE AUTHOR

Janet Carija Brandt lives in Indianapolis, Indiana, with her husband, two children, and assorted pets. She has worked with textiles in one way or another for the past twenty-five years and is tickled pink to be writing a book about WOW! appliqué quilts.

All About Wool

Using New Wool

The basic ingredient for a beautiful wool appliqué quilt or rug is beautiful wool. Your quilt or rug can be made completely from all new wool, all old wool, or a combination of both. Here are a few guidelines for starting your wool stockpile.

Shopping for new wool can be a challenge, depending on where you live and the time of year in which you shop. Wool isn't always available in all places, although more and more quilt shops are selling wool fabric. Support your local merchants first! However, if the fabric is not available locally, I have provided some mail-order sources at the back of the book for you.

The ideal wool is a tightly woven, 100% wool skirt or dress-weight fabric. When cut, tightly woven wool will not unravel easily along the edge. You are not as limited in your wool choices for wool appliqué as you are for rug hooking. Tight or loose weave, heavy-weight or lightweight, 100% wool or wool blend, new or old, plain weave or twill, solids, or plaids; all of these can be good options, so how do you choose?

Let's start with the first set of choices: tight weave or loose weave. Of all the choices, this is the one about which I am most particular. The tighter the weave, the easier it is to work with. If the fabric is 100% wool, even a very loose weave might be made usable by shrinking it (called felting) with repeated hot and cold cycles in the washing machine. If you love the color and

the weight of a loosely woven piece of wool, but shrinking doesn't work and you want to use it "no matter what," try spacing your blanket stitches a little closer together for an appliqué project or cutting your wool strips a little wider for a rug-hooking project.

When faced with all the various weights of wool fabric, look for medium-weight wool. Don't pass up the other weights though, if the color, weave, and fiber content are right. Lightweight wool makes a wonderful background fabric, but only when equally lightweight fabric is used for the appliqués. A heavyweight wool, on the other hand, can support light, medium, or heavyweight appliqués.

For rug hooking, cut the lightweight wool strips a little wider than what is normal for your rug and cut the heavier wool a little narrower than normal. (See "Rug-Hooking Techniques" on pages 67–71.)

Twills and tweeds are more difficult to work with than plain weaves, but what goodies you pass by if you don't at least try to use them! The solution here is the same as it was for a loosely woven wool; try to shrink the fabric. If you are successful, all the stray threads won't present problems, and you'll greatly increase your palette.

As for the question of using solids versus plaids, stripes, and checks, I love and use them all. Some purists think there is no place for patterned fabrics in a penny rug, insisting that they cheapen it. In my mind, the only things that cheapen any project are sloppy craftsmanship and truly inferior materials.

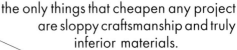

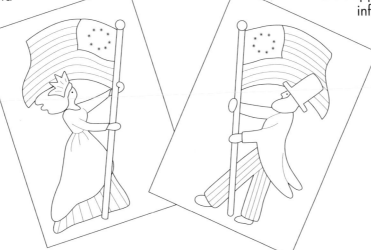

RECYCLING WOOL CLOTHING

Collecting old wool clothing to recycle into new wool appliqué quilts is great fun. Your neighbor's garage sale or your own closet are perfect places to begin your hunt. Thrift shops, such as the Salvation Army or Goodwill, are a wool picker's paradise. Enlist the help of friends who love to shop and hunt for bargains.

As you do for new wool, look for 100% wool. A skirt-weight wool or a wool flannel with a tight weave is great. Of course, there are exceptions here, too. If I find a skirt in an absolutely luscious color, and the weight and weave are right, but the fiber content label says it is not 100% wool, I might still go for it. I will go as low as 80% wool if it is perfect to use as it is; otherwise, I will not bother with it.

There are two reasons for this. First, if the weave is not tight enough originally, no amount of washing and drying a fabric blend will shrink it. Second, if I do want to change the color, a fabric blend will not take the dye as predictably or as evenly as a 100%-wool fabric. It just is not worth the trouble.

A 100% wool fabric takes up the dye more intensely than a wool blend.

I usually choose from the skirt rack when I shop. Slacks and jackets are too much work to take apart with only small pieces left for all the effort. As with new wool, choose solid colors, plaids, stripes, checks, and even tweeds. WOW! appliqué can incorporate any pattern and texture.

As soon as I get home with my wool treasures, I sort the skirts by color, and machine wash and dry them. (See "Washing Wool" below.) This serves three purposes. First, I now know I am working with clean fabric; second, the wools are now mothproof (moths love dirt, not wool); and third, the wool has probably shrunk slightly (felted) and is nice and soft. This makes the wool easier to work with.

Next, I cut off the waistbands and save the buttons. Many people save the zippers and the labels. I have seen some wonderful shirts and jackets with labels appliquéd all over them, but my thriftiness only extends to the buttons.

Last of all, I rip out the seams and hems, then step back and admire the soft, cuddly pile of wool.

WASHING WOOL

It is important to wash even new wool to shrink or felt it before you use it. For the purposes of WOW! quilts and hooked rugs, felted wool is any wool that has shrunk or become slightly matted so it does not easily unravel. This is usually achieved by simply machine washing and drying.

I throw the wool in the washing machine with a little detergent and use the warm and gentle cycle. I use regular laundry detergent with no bleach additives and add $\frac{1}{4}$ of a cup for a full load, less for a partial load. I use a hot and normal cycle if I want the fabric to be highly felted.

DYEING WOOL

Please don't skip this section. So many people are frightened by the subject, especially quilters who unsuccessfully tried to dye cotton, and have vowed to never try dyeing again. Dyeing wool is not like dyeing cotton—I know because I have tried both. I was discouraged with my first attempts at cotton dyeing and color setting but was delighted with my very first try at dyeing wool.

The biggest myth about dyeing is "It's so messy!" This is not necessarily true. Before I started dyeing, I had a very white kitchen. After dyeing a large volume of wool, I still have a very white kitchen, and I can assure you this has nothing to do with any great housekeeping skills!

The pans and utensils used for dyeing are not used for cooking. Keep them separate at all times. I move or cover all food-related items before I start and then cover the counters with newspaper.

Work in a well-ventilated area. Equipment you will need includes:

♥ One or more white enamel pans, 5-qt. size or larger. White pans work best, allowing you to see the color better than dark pans do. Use large pots for dyeing large pieces of wool. If the wool is too tightly packed in the dye pot, the resulting color will be uneven. (But it will be interesting and unique.)

♥ A large mixing spoon and tongs (Use any type of utensil except galvanized metal.)

♥ Aluminum foil for spot dyeing

♥ Pyrex pan (approximately 11" x 13") for spot dyeing

♥ Heavy rubber gloves for dip dyeing

♥ White vinegar (I buy the cheapest kind by the gallon.)

♥ Dyes (I use Cushing Perfection dyes.)

♥ Small measuring cups

♥ Small measuring spoons

♥ TOD (Triple Over Dye) measuring spoon (optional) (This is a special measuring spoon with a $\frac{1}{32}$ tsp. on one end and a $\frac{1}{4}$ tsp. on the other.)

Basic Dyeing Method

1. At least one hour before dyeing, presoak all wool in lukewarm water with just a few drops of liquid soap. This soaking moistens the fibers so they will take up the dye evenly. Sometimes, I toss the wool into a tub of water the night before so I know it has had plenty of time to soak. (I rinse out the soap when I rinse out the vinegar and excess dye at the end of the process.)

2. Fill the enamel pan about $\frac{3}{4}$ full of water. Bring to a boil.

3. Carefully measure your dyes into a small glass or plastic cup or pan, then add $\frac{1}{2}$ cup or so of boiling water to dissolve the dye. In this dyeing procedure, the amount of water is not important. The water just serves as a way of carrying the dye to the wool. The amount of dye in proportion to the amount of wool is what determines the final color.

4. After all of the dye is dissolved (there should be no more specks floating around), pour the solution into the large pot of boiling water. Stir well.

5. Now add the wool, stirring often.

6. After about five minutes, add $\frac{1}{2}$ cup vinegar to the dye pot. This helps the wool take up and keep the dye. Keep stirring gently. The more often you stir, the more even your color will be. Keep the water at a slow simmer.

7. Simmer the wool until all the dye is absorbed into the fabric and the water is clear, or until the desired color is reached. Remember, wet wool in the dye pot looks much darker than it will look when it is dry.

Dyeing equipment: enamel pot, spoon, tongs, dyes, measuring cups and spoons, white vinegar, and TOD measuring spoon

8. Remove the wool and rinse gently, first in hot water, then in gradually cooler water.
9. Hang or machine dry.

Now that wasn't so bad, was it? From this basic procedure, you can create all kinds of wonderful colors and effects. In addition to this, there is dip dyeing, spot dyeing, gradation dyeing, transitional dyeing, or the easiest of all, random dyeing.

Tips

- Remember, the more wool you dye, the more vinegar you need to set the color. If the wool does not seem to be taking up the color, add more vinegar (about ¼ cup at a time) and simmer longer.
- Each color of dye is made from a unique formula that may affect the way the wool takes the dye. For example, a piece of wool may take up the yellow part of a green dye more quickly than the blue part of the dye. If you remove the wool too soon, you will not get the full effect of the dye. Trying to dye the same color later will be difficult.

Dip Dyeing

For dip dyeing a piece of wool, such as the one needed for "Rise and Shine" on page 19, start with a well-soaked piece of wool, measuring approximately 11" x 14". To a large pot of boiling water, add dye (¹⁄₃₂ tsp. Buttercup Yellow for the "Rise and Shine" quilt) that has already been dissolved in a small amount of boiling water. Remember, it isn't the amount of water that determines the color; it is the proportion of dye to fabric.

Add ¼ cup of white vinegar to the dye pot and stir well. Wearing heavy rubber gloves (to protect your

fingers from the steam and boiling water), dip one of the short ends of the wool into the dye pot.

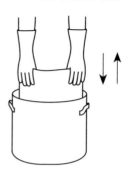

Keep the wool moving, dipping it in an up-and-down motion, so a solid line does not appear between the natural color of the wool and the dyed area. The lower edge of the wool (the edge in the dye pot) will become a nice, bright color (yellow in our example), fading into the natural color of the wool. If you wish, give the entire piece of wool one quick dip into the dyebath so a very subtle wash of color extends to the top edge. When all of the dye has been taken up by the wool or when you have obtained the color you want, set the wool aside.

In a fresh pot of boiling water, add another color of dye (¹⁄₃₂ tsp. of pink in our example) that has been dissolved in a small amount (¼ cup) of boiling water. Add ¼ cup of white vinegar to the boiling water and dye mixture.

Now, repeat the dipping procedure, this time putting the opposite end of the wool into the dye pot. Gently dip the wool in an up-and-down motion until the color is bright on the bottom and gently blends and mixes with the color on top.

Remember to always keep the wool gently moving up and down so that a solid line of dye does not appear in the middle of your wool. When you have the color you want (keep in mind that wet wool is much darker than dry wool), or all of the dye is taken up from the dye pot, rinse the wool in hot, then warm, and finally cool water to remove the soap and vinegar. Line or machine dry.

Gradation Dyeing

This method provides several pieces of wool, each slightly darker than the next, but all the same color. Prepare several dyebaths, using the same color of dye, but for each dyebath, add a slightly stronger concentration of dye. For example, you might try adding $\frac{1}{32}$ tsp. for the first dyebath, $\frac{1}{16}$ tsp. for the second, $\frac{3}{32}$ tsp. for the third, and $\frac{1}{8}$ tsp. for the fourth dyebath. Dye one piece of wool per dyebath.

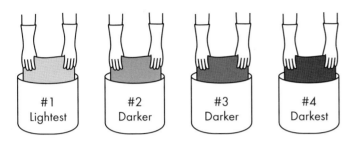

Transitional Dyeing

This method also involves dyeing several pieces of wool, this time changing the dye from one color to another, for example, from pink to purple. The first dyebath contains only pink dye, so the piece of wool dyed in it is pure pink. For the second dyebath, use the same total amount of dye, but use a little less pink and a small amount of purple. The resulting pink piece has just a tiny hint of purple. If the third dyebath contains equal amounts of pink and purple dye, and the fourth dyebath contains the reverse amounts of dye as the second dyebath, the resulting pieces will be more and more purple. If you dye the last piece in a pure purple dyebath, you will have a gradation of wool pieces from one hue to the next. You can have any number of swatches of wool, any ratio, and any combination of dye colors. Experiment to achieve even gradations of colors. Remember to add vinegar to the dyebaths to fix the color.

Spot Dyeing

Spot dyeing gives unusual, unpredictable, but always fun results. Due to the concentrations and different colors of dye in different areas of a single piece of wool, you will obtain light and dark areas as well as several colors within the same piece.

1. Presoak the wool in water and vinegar.
2. Line the bottom of a shallow Pyrex baking dish with crumpled aluminum foil. Place crumpled wet wool on top of the foil. Keep the wool in a single, but not smooth layer.

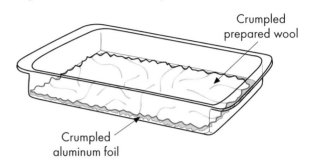

Crumpled prepared wool

Crumpled aluminum foil

3. Dissolve each color of dye with approximately $\frac{1}{4}$ cup of boiling water. For each piece of wool, I find that a total of two or three different colors usually works best.

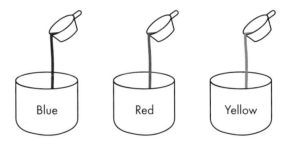

Blue   Red   Yellow

4. Spoon small amounts of each dye color over the wool in a random pattern.

5. Carefully add just enough boiling water at the edge of the wool to keep the wool moist but not swimming in lots of water. Too much water will make the colors run together and turn muddy; not enough will cause the wool to dry out and possibly burn in the oven.

6. Cover the pan with foil and steam in the oven for 30 minutes at 250°F. Check occasionally to make sure the wool has not dried out. Cool, rinse, and dry.

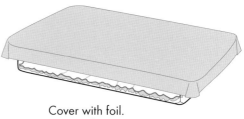

Cover with foil.
Steam at 250°F for 30 minutes.

Random Dyeing

For this method, include pieces of several different wools (different colors, patterns, and/or textures) in the same dyebath. The reason for doing this is similar to the reason quilters tea-dye fabrics. All of the resulting colors will work together, whether they are soft and pastel or strong and dark.

Random dyeing works best when making a pictorial-type hooked rug, such as "Red Hen," on page 56. By using eight different recycled wools and five different dye-color combinations, I came up with over forty colors of wool to use for hooking the rug. In a nonsymmetrical rug of this type, the colors do not need to match perfectly from one side of the rug to the other.

Dyeing transforms eight dull recycled wools into a rainbow of new shades.

When working on an Oriental or symmetrical design, carefully measure the wool and the dye so you can create the same color again if you run out of wool. Keeping notes and records as you work provides valuable backup information later.

1. Begin by tearing your wool into pieces that are easy to handle. If you rip or tear your wool, you will get perfectly straight edges. You will also know where the grain line is.

2. If you are dyeing a piece of wool for the background of a WOW! quilt, tear the wool the size of the finished piece plus a couple of inches for shrinkage.

3. Prepare and dye the wool using the "Basic Dyeing Method" on pages 7-8. After rinsing and gently squeezing the water out of the wool, you will have a pretty good idea of the final color. Do you want lighter tints? Either add more wool or less dye next time. Do you want darker shades? Either add less wool or more dye.

Tip

If you like the color of your wool before the water is clear, you can remove the wool after you have added the vinegar. Toss another piece of presoaked wool into the remaining dye, add a little more vinegar (1/4 cup), and simmer until clear. This second batch probably will not be as dark as the first but will coordinate perfectly and can be used to great advantage in shading different designs.

Keep in mind that the original color of the wool will also make a difference in the final color. Light colors show the dye more readily than dark colors.

See how simple it is? You can of course experiment with any color combination you like. You really cannot make a mistake. The color that you think is ugly today may be the exact shade you are looking for tomorrow.

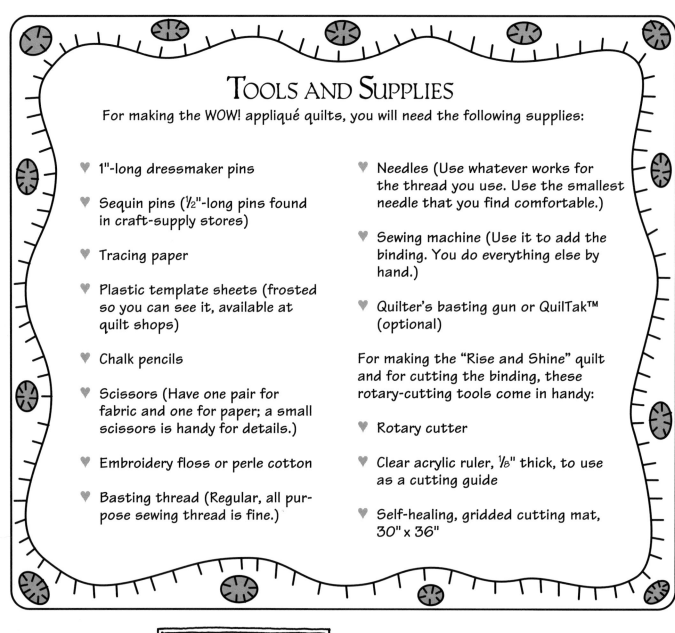

TOOLS AND SUPPLIES

For making the WOW! appliqué quilts, you will need the following supplies:

- ♥ 1"-long dressmaker pins

- ♥ Sequin pins (½"-long pins found in craft-supply stores)

- ♥ Tracing paper

- ♥ Plastic template sheets (frosted so you can see it, available at quilt shops)

- ♥ Chalk pencils

- ♥ Scissors (Have one pair for fabric and one for paper; a small scissors is handy for details.)

- ♥ Embroidery floss or perle cotton

- ♥ Basting thread (Regular, all purpose sewing thread is fine.)

- ♥ Needles (Use whatever works for the thread you use. Use the smallest needle that you find comfortable.)

- ♥ Sewing machine (Use it to add the binding. You do everything else by hand.)

- ♥ Quilter's basting gun or QuilTak™ (optional)

For making the "Rise and Shine" quilt and for cutting the binding, these rotary-cutting tools come in handy:

- ♥ Rotary cutter

- ♥ Clear acrylic ruler, ⅛" thick, to use as a cutting guide

- ♥ Self-healing, gridded cutting mat, 30" x 36"

Wool Appliqué and Quilting Techniques

TRANSFERRING PATTERNS

There are three possible ways to transfer the design patterns for the wool appliqué projects in this book.

Method 1: For simple shapes that will be used only once or twice, I recommend using tracing paper to make templates. Trace the pattern from the book onto tracing paper, cut out the pattern, then pin the pattern to the wool. Cut out the wool piece. *Do not add seam allowances to either the paper or the wool appliqué pieces.*

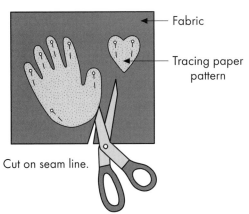

Fabric

Tracing paper pattern

Cut on seam line.

Don't try to cut the paper and the wool at the same time. Your scissors won't like it, and the edges of both the paper and the wool will be ragged. (Blanket stitches will not hide poorly cut edges.) Sharp scissors and careful craftsmanship go a long way at this stage.

Method 2: This pattern-transfer method requires making plastic templates. Use the lightweight template plastic sold in quilt shops or a similar-weight plastic. Trace the pattern from the book onto the plastic sheet and cut out the template. Do not add seam allowances. Using a chalk pencil, draw around the template

on the wool. You must hold the template very firmly because the wool has a tendency to stretch and pull under the plastic. Cut the wool on the chalk line.

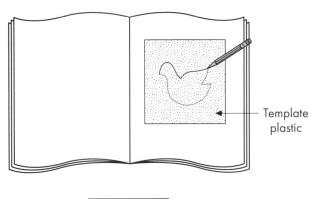

Template plastic

Method 3: For pattern pieces that are highly detailed or that will be used many times, I recommend using a lightweight, nonfusible interfacing for the template. Trace the pattern from the book directly onto the interfacing. Cut out the interfacing, pin the interfacing to the wool, and cut out the wool piece. Remove the interfacing when you have finished cutting out the wool.

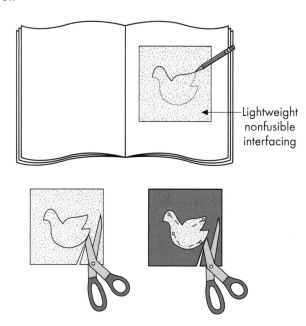

Lightweight nonfusible interfacing

Note: The ray pattern of the "Rise and Shine" quilt on page 19 is an exception to this rule of thumb. Cut the interfacing and wool together. See page 20.

STITCHING

The blanket stitch is the most commonly used stitch for all of the WOW! quilts. Pin or baste the appliqué piece in place, then stitch. Be sure to catch both the appliqué and the background layers of fabric with each stitch.

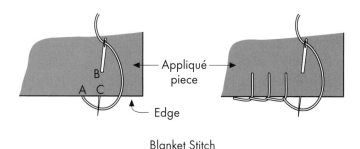

Appliqué piece

Edge

Blanket Stitch

Try to keep your stitches in uniform proportions throughout the piece. If you begin by making your stitches tall and close, keep that same proportion even on a smaller appliqué piece.

Try for:

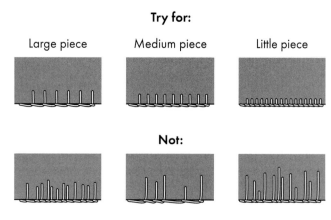

Large piece   Medium piece   Little piece

Not:

Other stitches used for embellishment are the chain stitch, lazy-daisy stitch, running stitch, embroidered star, satin stitch, French knot, and the fly-stitch variation.

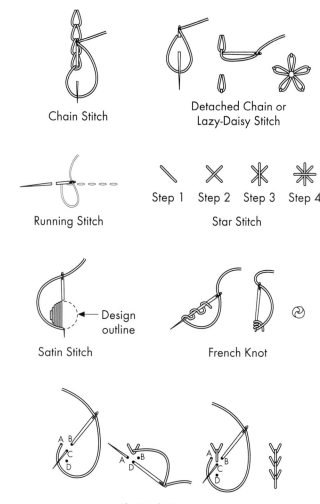

Chain Stitch

Detached Chain or Lazy-Daisy Stitch

Running Stitch

Step 1   Step 2   Step 3   Step 4

Star Stitch

Design outline

Satin Stitch

French Knot

Fly Stitch Variation

INITIALING YOUR WORK

Have you ever been faced with a box of old photos with no names and no dates on the back? At the time you took the pictures, you were sure you would never forget that information. Now you can't remember and you can be certain no one else will know either! That also happens to quilts and rugs. What a shame it is!

As timidly or as boldly as you wish, please include your name or initials and the date on your work. It makes the piece unique, special, and identifiable. For a hooked rug, I add my initials and date to the pattern with a permanent waterproof marker *before* I hook. This way, I won't forget to hook it in as I work.

For the WOW! quilts, add the initials and date almost any time. For me, the best time is after all of the appliquéing is done, but before it is quilted. That way, I can quilt around the letters and the numbers, too, incorporating them into the design.

I like to sign my quilts with chain-stitch letters, but any embroidery stitch you are comfortable with will work. (See "Stitching" on page 14.) I embroider the letters and numbers freehand, letting them go where the needle leads me. If you prefer, draw them with chalk pencil, then embroider them.

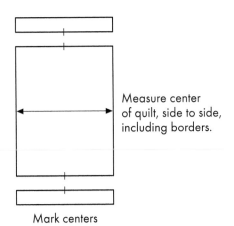

ADDING BORDERS

When adding borders to your quilt, measure through the center of the quilt from side to side and cut the top and bottom borders to this measurement. Matching the center and ends of each border with the center and the ends of the quilt, pin, then sew each border to the quilt.

Measure center of quilt, side to side, including borders.

Mark centers

Measure through the center of the quilt from top to bottom, including the borders you just added and cut each side border to this measurement. Matching centers and ends, pin, then sew a border to each side of the quilt. Adding the borders in this manner prevents wavy borders or distorted quilt centers.

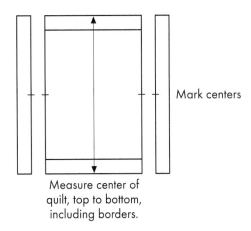

Mark centers

Measure center of quilt, top to bottom, including borders.

FINISHING THE QUILT

Batting

I always use Hobbs Thermore® batting "made especially for quilted clothing." Because it is so thin, it is easy to quilt with the wool on top and the cotton backing on the bottom. I cut the batting $1/4$" larger than the quilt top on all four sides. I like to see the batting edge as I quilt so I know that I am not skipping a spot.

Backing

I choose most of my backing fabrics from standard-weight, 100% cottons sold for quiltmaking. I cut the backing the same size as the batting. For all backing fabrics, be sure to prewash and dry the fabric before using.

Layering and Basting

On a flat surface, lay out the backing fabric first, with the wrong side up. Place the batting over this, making sure the edges line up. Finally, with the right side up, place the quilt top on the batting.

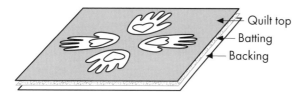

Quilt top
Batting
Backing

With 1"-long dressmaking pins, a basting gun, or a needle and thread, baste the three layers together. Pin or baste closely in areas that will not be quilted.

Quilting

The folk embroideries of Eastern Europe have always had a strong influence on my work. I think my quilting stitch reflects that. The length of the stitch or the number of stitches per inch are not what is important to me. I am most concerned with the color and the texture that the patterns create. If it takes double thread and large stitches to achieve the right effect, then that is what I do!

Sometimes I want long stitches to accent a design element. Other times, I try for lots of tiny stitches to create a dimpled background. For this type of quilt, if you are happy with the effect, then that is the right stitch!

If you wish to mark the quilting lines, use chalk or the marker of your choice. Remember to test your marker on a scrap to make sure you can remove the marks. Quilt your WOW! quilts with two or three strands of embroidery floss or a single strand of perle cotton.

1. Make a small knot at the end of your quilting thread. Insert the needle into the quilt top about $1/2$" away from where you plan to begin quilting. Pull the needle through the batting and bring it up at the point where you want to begin the line of quilting.

2. Gently pull the knot through the top fabric, leaving it buried in the batting.

3. Using a running stitch, quilt along the line to be quilted. WOW! quilting stitches can be as large or as small as you like.

4. When you reach the end of your stitching, make a small knot close to the quilt and pop it through the top fabric into the batting. Bring the end of the thread out about $1/2$" from where the thread went into the quilt and clip it.

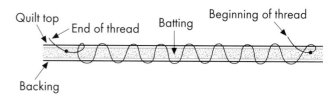

Quilt top
End of thread
Batting
Beginning of thread
Backing

I begin my quilting in the center of the quilt and echo the shapes as I find them. Because I don't work with a hoop, I tend to draw the stitches up fairly tight, an effect I like. This slightly reduces the size of the quilt.

Squaring the Top

After I have finished the quilting, but before I add the binding, I like to "square up" the quilt. This simply means that each of the quilt's four corners is 90°. This is one of the times when a gridded cutting mat is indispensable. Most of these quilts are small enough so they will fit on a mat with room to spare. I work on a 30" x 36" mat.

To square a quilt, trim the smoothest and straightest edge of the quilt, using a rotary cutter, clear acrylic cutting guide, and gridded cutting mat.

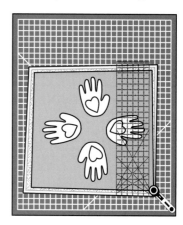

Then place this cut edge along one of the grid lines on the cutting mat, lining up the next edge with a perpendicular line on the mat, and trim the second edge.

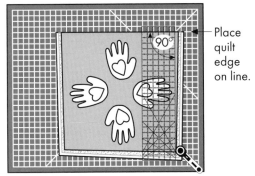

Place quilt edge on line.

The corner between these two cut edges is now 90°, or "square." Continue lining up the edges and trimming in this manner until all the corners are square.

Binding

For most of the quilts in this book, a straight-grain binding is sufficient. For quilts with rounded or irregular edges, I recommend using bias-grain binding for a smoothly finished edge. For "Petal Hearts" on page 57, I used a purchased ½"-wide, double-fold, bias-tape binding, since the background of the quilt is black and most of the edge is hidden by the petals.

For all straight-grain binding, I use 1½"-wide strips of cotton. You can use wool, but it is bulky. For the "Folksy Tree Skirt" on page 36, I wanted a narrower edge and used 1¼"-wide bias strips for the binding.

To make straight-grain binding, cut strips across the width of the fabric, from selvage to selvage. Stitch strips together, end to end, to make one continuous strip of binding.

To make bias-grain binding, I frequently use "fat quarters" (18" x 22"). Press the fabric, making sure the edges are on the straight grain (the threads that run parallel to the cut edge).

1. Fold over one corner of the fabric diagonally to find the "true bias" (the line that runs at a 45° angle to the straight grain).

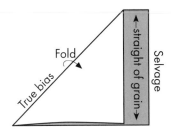

Fold
True bias
straight of grain
Selvage

2. Cut along this fold line, then use it as a guide to rotary cut the number of 1¼"-wide strips needed to bind the quilt.

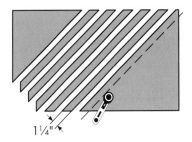

1¼"

3. Stitch the pieces together as shown to make one continuous bias strip. Press the seams open.

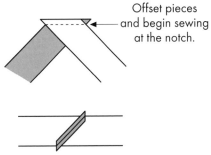

Offset pieces and begin sewing at the notch.

Sewing the Binding to the Quilt

1. With right sides together, line up the raw edges of the binding and the quilt top. Fold the beginning of the binding back ½" over itself and pin in place as shown. Stitch, using a ¼"-wide seam allowance, along one side of the quilt, stopping ¼" from the edge. Backstitch and clip the threads.

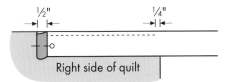

½" ¼"
Right side of quilt

2. Remove the quilt from the machine. Fold the binding away from the quilt, perpendicular to the edge you just stitched, then fold it back down along the next edge to be stitched.

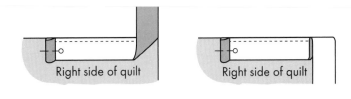

Right side of quilt   Right side of quilt

3. Starting at the top, stitch down the next side until you come within ¼" from the next edge. Backstitch.

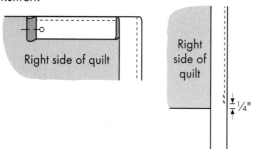

4. Repeat the corner turns. After you have stitched the binding to the quilt all the way around, overlap the binding about ¼" over the fold at the beginning. Trim off the extra binding, then finish stitching the binding to the quilt.

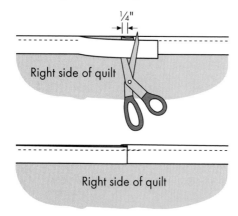

5. Turn the binding over to the back of the quilt and fold under ¼" along the raw edge. Pin and slipstitch in place. This hem will cover the machine stitching, and the corners will form folded miters.

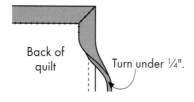

Steam Pressing

At a recent quilt show, I passed a vendor's booth filled with miniature quilts. They were lovely quilts, but not one of them had been pressed. They seemed to droop and sag instead of being the perky bits of art they could have been. I thought it was such a shame that what should have been a stunning exhibit was instead only mediocre.

A final steam pressing gives the quilt a crisp finish that I find attractive. Here are a few steps for giving your quilts that professional finish.

To steam press, I use a large piece of muslin that is only slightly damp. Wring it out well—it should not be dripping wet.

Place your WOW! quilt on the ironing board, right side down. Cover with the damp cloth. Press, with the iron set at "wool." Gently move the iron around the press cloth, being careful not to stretch or distort the quilt. A steam iron is not necessary, since the damp cloth will provide all of the steam necessary. I press just until the press cloth is dry.

Remove the cloth and allow the quilt to cool on the ironing board or other flat surface for about 5 to 10 minutes, or until completely cool and dry.

GENERAL QUILT TIPS

♥ Where more than one color is used for the background of a quilt, the measurements given include a ¼"-wide seam allowance. Unless otherwise indicated, sew all seams with ¼"-wide seam allowances.

♥ My favorite thimble is a rubber finger guard sold at the local office-supply store!

♥ Sew around all of the edges of an appliquéd piece, even the parts that are partially covered by other pattern pieces. This helps the wool pieces lie flatter.

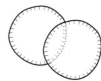

Wow! Appliqué Quilts

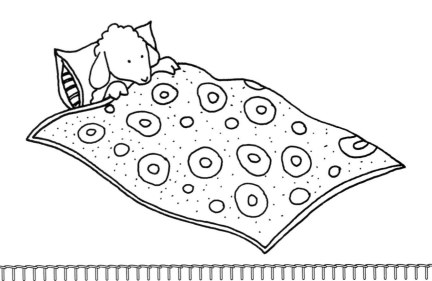

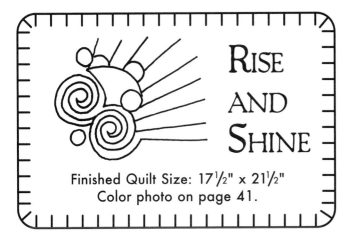

RISE AND SHINE

Finished Quilt Size: 17½" x 21½"
Color photo on page 41.

Art Deco design has fascinated me for a long time. During the 1970s, there was a wonderful Art Deco–inspired store in London, called Biba. As a college student, I couldn't afford to buy anything except a postcard and a snack from the food hall. I still have the postcard and the bag that the snack came in, each framed and hanging in my home. And now, I have a WOW! quilt to add to my collection.

Materials

Dimensions given are for prewashed wool pieces. Refer to "All About Wool," beginning on page 5, for selecting and dyeing wool before starting this project. The fabric measurements indicate minimum amounts required for all pieces except the background. Cotton yardage is based on 44"-wide fabric.

11" x 14" rectangle for radiating rays*
7" x 7" squares of 4 or 5 assorted colors for swirls and circles
17½" x 21½" rectangle for background
½ yd. cotton for backing and binding
19" x 23" rectangle of lightweight batting
Coordinating embroidery floss or perle cotton

*I used a dip-dyed piece of wool, in which the color changes from one end of the rectangle to the other. (See "Dip Dyeing" on page 8.)

Cutting and Assembly

Note: For this pattern, I strongly recommend using a lightweight, nonfusible interfacing for the patterns.

1. **RAY PATTERN:** Trace the Art Deco Ray Pattern from the pullout pattern onto the interfacing all in one piece. *Do not cut it into pieces.* Pin the interfacing pattern to the wool, placing the pins in the blank areas and making sure that they do not cross the lines. With a rotary cutter and a straight edge, cut along the lines, cutting the interfacing pattern and the wool at the same time.

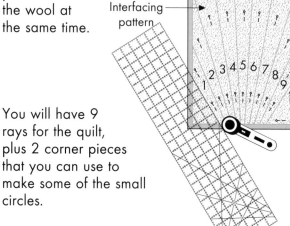

Wool
Interfacing pattern

You will have 9 rays for the quilt, plus 2 corner pieces that you can use to make some of the small circles.

2. **SWIRL PATTERNS:** The interfacing method works well for the swirl patterns too, but this time, cut out the interfacing pattern before pinning it to the wool. Pin with sequin pins. Cut out the wool swirls.

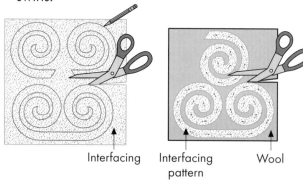

Interfacing   Interfacing pattern   Wool

3. Using the templates on pages 75–76, trace the remaining patterns and prepare the pieces for appliqué. (See "Wool Appliqué and Quilting Techniques" on pages 13–15.)

4. Arrange rays on the backing fabric. I find it easiest to mark the top center of the background and, starting with ray #5, arrange the strips from the center out to each side. Align the outside edge of each ray with the edge of the background.

Center top

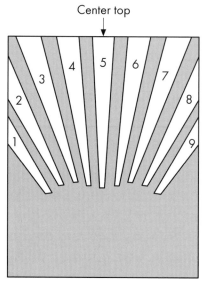

Note: The rays' lower points will be too long but do not trim them yet; wait until outer swirls O and P and pieces I, J, K, and K reversed are in place, then cut them.

5. Pin the remaining prepared wool pieces to the background fabric, referring to the quilt diagram below for placement. Do not pin small circles to pieces I, J, K, and K reversed.

6. Appliqué all of the edges of the pinned pieces except the tops of pieces I, J, K, and K reversed.

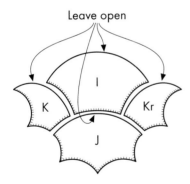

7. Now arrange the small circles on pieces I, J, K, and K reversed, tucking some under the unsewn edges as shown. Appliqué everything in place, including the top edges of I, J, K, and K reversed.

8. Using the embroidery stitches of your choice, initial and date the front of your quilt. (See "Initialing Your Work" on page 15.)

Finishing the Quilt

Refer to the directions given for finishing the quilt on pages 15–18.

1. Layer the quilt top with batting and backing. Pin or baste the 3 layers together.
2. Quilt as desired, using embroidery floss or perle cotton.
3. Press the back of the quilt, placing a damp cloth between the quilt and the iron.
4. Square up the quilt.
5. Bind the edges.
6. Give the back side of the quilt one final steam pressing.

Flowers and Hearts

Finished Quilt Size: 10" x 13"
Color photos on pages 42 and 43.

This is the WOW! quilt that started it all for me. The heart-in-hand motif is found in many cultures throughout history. To me, it symbolizes how near and dear we must always hold life and love.

The materials needed for this quilt are just a little of this and a little of that, so getting started is easy.

Materials

Dimensions given are for prewashed wool pieces. Refer to "All About Wool," beginning on page 5, for selecting and dyeing wool before starting this project. The fabric measurements indicate minimum amounts required for all pieces except the background. Cotton yardage is based on 44"-wide fabric.

10" x 13" rectangle for background
4" x 9" rectangle for hands
2" x 6" strip for hearts
2" x 3" rectangle each for flowers A, B, and H
4" x 5" rectangle for light leaves C and I
4" x 5" rectangle for dark leaves D and J
3" x 5" rectangle for flowers E
2" x 4" rectangle each for flowers F and G
⅓ yd. coordinating cotton for backing and binding
11" x 14" rectangle of lightweight batting
Coordinating embroidery floss or perle cotton

Cutting and Assembly

1. Using the templates on page 76, trace the patterns and prepare the pieces for appliqué. (See "Wool Appliqué and Quilting Techniques" on pages 13–15.)
2. Pin prepared wool pieces to the background fabric, referring to the quilt diagram on page 23 for placement.

3. Working from the bottom to the top layers and using 3 strands of embroidery floss, appliqué hands, hearts, leaves C, D, I, and J, and flowers A, B, E, F, G, and H. Use a blanket stitch for all pieces except flowers B, F, and H. Appliqué these flowers, using a chain stitch around the edges. (See "Stitching" on page 14.)

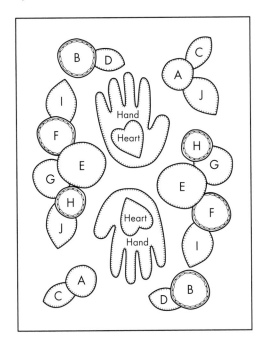

4. Embroider flower centers B, F, and H with chain stitches. Embroider flower centers E with a lazy-daisy stitch, embroider leaves C and I with a fly-stitch variation, and center veins on leaves D and J with a chain stitch. (See "Stitching" on page 14.)

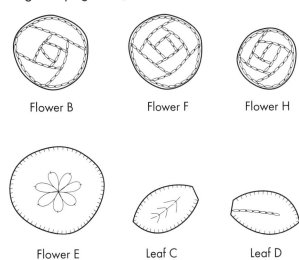

Flower B Flower F Flower H

Flower E Leaf C Leaf D

5. Using the embroidery stitches of your choice, initial and date the front of your quilt. (See "Initialing Your Work" on page 15.)

Finishing the Quilt

Refer to the directions given for finishing the quilt on pages 15–18.

1. Layer the quilt top with batting and backing. Pin or baste the 3 layers together.
2. Quilt as desired, using embroidery floss or perle cotton.
3. Press the back of the quilt, placing a damp cloth between the quilt and the iron.
4. Square up the quilt.
5. Bind the edges.
6. Give the back side of the quilt one final steam pressing.

Tip

Leave the other pieces pinned in place as much as possible as you work. Remove pins or turn back only those parts of the appliqué pieces that are in the way of your stitching.

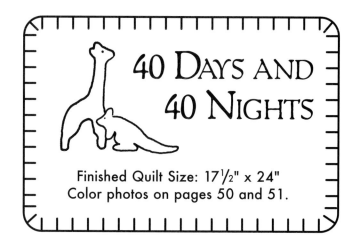

40 Days and 40 Nights

Finished Quilt Size: 17½" x 24"
Color photos on pages 50 and 51.

This is a delightfully simple representation of the story of Noah's Ark. The light side of this two-colored background represents cloudy, rainy days. The dark side represents the cloudy, rainy nights. Choose either a solid or a print for the background if you wish.

If you plan to embroider the words "40 days" and "40 nights" on the border of your quilt, I recommend using a plaid or check fabric for the border. That way guidelines for the lettering are built right in!

Materials

Dimensions given are for prewashed wool pieces. Refer to "All About Wool," beginning on page 5, for selecting and dyeing wool before starting this project. The fabric measurements indicate minimum amounts required for all pieces except the background. Cotton yardage is based on 44"-wide fabric.

10" x 13" rectangle of light for background
10" x 13" rectangle of dark for background
5" x 10" rectangles (at least 7 colors) of assorted colors for animals and ark
12" x 22" rectangle for border
⅝ yd. coordinating cotton for backing and binding
19" x 25" rectangle of lightweight batting
Coordinating embroidery floss or perle cotton

Cutting and Assembly

1. Using the templates on pages 77–78, trace the patterns and prepare the pieces for appliqué. (See "Wool Appliqué and Quilting Techniques" on pages 13–15.)
2. Pin prepared wool pieces to the background fabric, referring to the quilt diagram on page 24 for placement.
3. With 2 or 3 strands of embroidery floss, appliqué the animals to the background, using the blanket stitch. (See "Stitching" on page 14.)
4. Appliqué the window section of the ark, then the upper and lower portions. (Or cut the ark from a single piece of fabric.) Appliqué the doorway, then the gangplank.

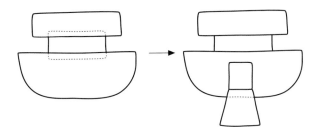

5. Using 3 strands of embroidery floss and the satin stitch, embroider Noah and the windows. If you like, embroider the animals' eyes with French knots. (See "Stitching" on page 14.)

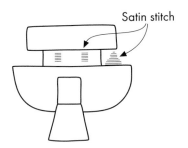

Satin stitch

6. From border fabric, cut 4 strips, each 2½" wide. Following the directions for adding borders, measure, cut, and add top and bottom borders to the quilt. Measure, cut, and add side borders to the quilt. (See "Adding Borders" on page 15.)
7. Chain-stitch "40 days" and "40 nights" around the border, using the lettering template on page 77. I did this embroidery freehand to give the letters a folksy feel.
8. Using the embroidery stitches of your choice, initial and date the front of your quilt. (See "Initialing Your Work" on page 15.)

Finishing the Quilt

Refer to the directions given for finishing the quilt on pages 15–18.

1. Layer the quilt top with batting and backing. Pin or baste the 3 layers together.
2. Quilt as desired, using embroidery floss or perle cotton.
3. Press the back of the quilt, placing a damp cloth between the quilt and the iron.
4. Square up the quilt.
5. Bind the edges.
6. Give the back side of the quilt one final steam pressing.

PINK BIRD

Finished Quilt Size: 13¼" x 20¾"
Color photo on page 44.

I based this fun quilt on a whimsical hooked rug that I designed. I named the bird "Phoebe." She lives on the planet Pluto, residing in a large red house with brightly illuminated windows! She eats the delicious fruit growing near her home and is a very happy bird.

Materials

Dimensions given are for prewashed wool pieces. Refer to "All About Wool," beginning on page 5, for selecting and dyeing wool before starting this project. The fabric measurements indicate minimum amounts required for all pieces except the background. Cotton yardage is based on 44"-wide fabric.

11" x 13¼" rectangle for sky
10¼" x 13¼" rectangle for ground
15" x 20" rectangle for trees
8" x 10" rectangle for house and path
4" x 4" square for windows, door, and moon
6" x 12" rectangle for clouds
5" x 5" square for bird
5" x 5" square for fruit
⅝ yd. coordinating cotton for backing and binding
13" x 15" rectangle of lightweight batting
Coordinating embroidery floss or perle cotton

Cutting and Assembly

1. Placing sky and ground pieces right sides together, sew along the 13¼" edge with a ¼"-wide seam.

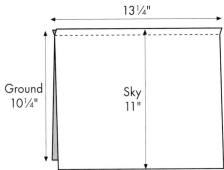

2. Using the templates on pages 79–81 and on the pullout pattern, trace the patterns and prepare the pieces for appliqué. (See "Wool Appliqué and Quilting Techniques" on pages 13–15.)

3. Pin prepared wool pieces to the background fabric, referring to the quilt diagram below for placement.

4. Using the blanket stitch, appliqué the pieces in numerical order, then appliqué the fruit. (See "Stitching" on page 14.)

5. Using the embroidery stitches of your choice, initial and date the front of your quilt. (See "Initialing Your Work" on page 15.)

Finishing the Quilt

Refer to the directions given for finishing the quilt on pages 15–18.

1. Layer the quilt top with batting and backing. Pin or baste the 3 layers together.
2. Quilt as desired, using embroidery floss or perle cotton.
3. Press the back of the quilt, placing a damp cloth between the quilt and the iron.
4. Square up the quilt.
5. Bind the edges.
6. Give the back side of the quilt one final steam pressing.

UNCLE SAM

Finished Quilt Size: 10" x 14"
Color photos on pages 46 and 47.

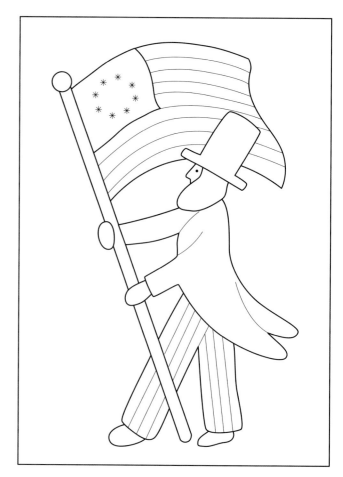

This quilt and the quilt on pages 30–31 represent a patriotic duo, Uncle Sam and Lady Liberty. Uncle Sam is dressed in his snappy navy blue tails and striped red pants. I embroidered the stripes on his pants and on the flag with chain stitches. The stripes could also be appliquéd.

Materials

Dimensions given are for prewashed wool pieces. Refer to "All About Wool," beginning on page 5, for selecting and dyeing wool before starting this project. The fabric measurements indicate minimum amounts required for all pieces except the background. Cotton yardage is based on 44"-wide fabric.

10" x 14" rectangle for background
8" x 10" rectangle for flag and pants
4" x 13" rectangle for top hat, jacket, shoes, flag corner, and pole
3" x 3" square for face and hands
2" x 2" square for beard
1" x 1" square for brass knob on pole
⅓ yd. coordinating cotton for backing and binding
11" x 15" rectangle of lightweight batting
Coordinating embroidery floss or perle cotton

Cutting and Assembly

1. Using the templates on pages 81–82 and on the pullout pattern, trace the patterns and prepare the pieces for appliqué. The pattern for the flagpole is on the pullout pattern. (See "Wool Appliqué and Quilting Techniques" on pages 13–15.)
2. Pin prepared wool pieces to the background fabric, referring to the quilt diagram above for placement.
3. Using a blanket stitch, appliqué pieces to the quilt in the order given or in the order of your choice. I began with Uncle Sam's shoes and then added his pants, jacket (leaving the end of the lower sleeve free for tucking under the hand later), face, and beard. I appliquéd the

flag, tucking Sam's top hat out of the way when I came to it, the corner of the flag, then the hat.

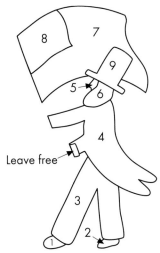

Leave free

4. Appliqué the flagpole, hands, and finally the brass knob at the end of the pole. Finish appliquéing the lower sleeve.

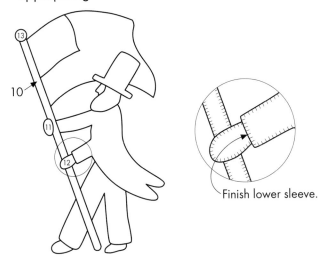

Finish lower sleeve.

5. With a chalk pencil or similar marker, draw in the lines for the flag's stripes and for the stripes on Uncle Sam's pants. For the flag's stripes, embroider 4 rows of chain stitches for each stripe. For the pants, embroider 1 row of chain stitches for each stripe. (See "Stitching" on page 14.)

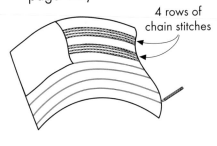

4 rows of chain stitches

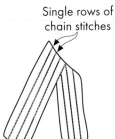

Single rows of chain stitches

6. For the flag's stars, I found a very simple way to mark their location. Using 1"-long straight pins, I arranged the pins in the center of the flag corner as shown and embroidered a star stitch at both ends of each pin.

7. Embroider a French knot for Uncle Sam's eye.
8. Using the embroidery stitches of your choice, initial and date the front of your quilt. (See "Initialing Your Work" on page 15.)

Finishing the Quilt

Refer to the directions given for finishing the quilt on pages 15–18.

1. Layer the quilt top with batting and backing. Pin or baste the 3 layers together.
2. Quilt as desired, using embroidery floss or perle cotton, or cut star shapes out of any scrap fabric and scatter around the background of the quilt. Pin the stars in place but do not appliqué—use the fabric stars only as guides. Quilt around the stars, Uncle Sam, and the flag. Remove the fabric stars after quilting.

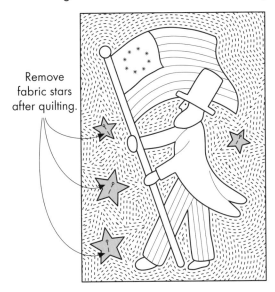

Remove fabric stars after quilting.

3. Press the back of the quilt, placing a damp cloth between the quilt and the iron.
4. Square up the quilt.
5. Bind the edges.
6. Give the back side of the quilt one final steam pressing.

LADY LIBERTY

Finished Quilt Size: 10" x 14"
Color photos on pages 46 and 47.

As I worked on this quilt and the Uncle Sam quilt on pages 28-29, I nicknamed them Libby and Sam. I have used Lady Liberty in several different designs. (See the Stars and Stripes quilt and Miss Freedom hooked rug in the Gallery on page 54.) Here, she is Uncle Sam's counterpart. The two balanced designs work together, so you can combine them in one quilt if you like.

Materials

Dimensions given are for prewashed wool pieces. Refer to "All About Wool," beginning on page 5, for selecting and dyeing wool before starting this project. The fabric measurements indicate minimum amounts required for all pieces except the background. Cotton yardage is based on 44"-wide fabric.

10" x 14" rectangle for background
8" x 10" rectangle for dress and flag
7" x 13" rectangle for flag corner, hair, pole, and lower skirt
3" x 3" square for crown and brass knob on pole
3" x 3" for face and hands
⅓ yd. coordinating cotton for backing and binding
11" x 15" rectangle of lightweight batting
Coordinating embroidery floss or perle cotton

Cutting and Assembly

1. Using the templates on pages 83 and 84 and on the pullout pattern, trace the patterns and prepare the pieces for appliqué. The pattern for the flagpole is on the pullout pattern. (See "Wool Appliqué and Quilting Techniques" on pages 13–15.)
2. Pin prepared wool pieces to the background fabric, referring to the quilt diagram above for placement.

3. Using a blanket stitch, appliqué pieces to the quilt in the order given or in the order of your choice. (See "Stitching" on page 14.) Appliqué the lower skirt, face, flag, and flag corner, hair, crown, and dress, leaving the sleeves free to insert the hands under them.

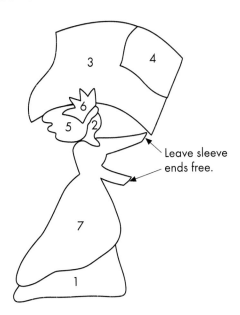

Leave sleeve ends free.

4. Appliqué the flagpole and hands, making sure that the hands fit naturally around the pole. Appliqué the sleeve ends and the brass knob at the end of the flagpole.

5. With a chalk pencil or similar marker, draw in the lines for the flag's stripes. Draw the crown, dress details, and stripes on Lady Liberty's dress and lower skirt, referring to the template for placement. For the flag's stripes, embroider 4 rows of chain stitches for each stripe. (See step 5 on page 29 for the Uncle Sam quilt.) For the crown, dress, and each stripe on the lower skirt, embroider 1 row of chain stitches.

6. Refer to step 6 of the cutting and assembly instructions at the top of page 29 for embroidering the flag's stars.

7. Embroider a French knot for Lady Liberty's eye.

8. Using the embroidery stitches of your choice, initial and date the front of your quilt. (See "Initialing Your Work" on page 15.)

Finishing the Quilt

Refer to the directions given for finishing the quilt on pages 15–18.

1. Layer the quilt top with batting and backing. Pin or baste the 3 layers together.

2. Quilt as desired, using embroidery floss or perle cotton, or use the same technique described for the Uncle Sam quilt in step 2 of "Finishing the Quilt" on page 29.

3. Press the back of the quilt, placing a damp cloth between the quilt and the iron.

4. Square up the quilt.

5. Bind the edges.

6. Give the back side of the quilt one final steam pressing.

MOONLIGHT TREE

Finished Quilt Size: 10" x 14"
Color photos on page 45.

Who can resist the beauty of any moonlit scene? Try using dark colors for the tree, fruit, and birds, then setting them against an even darker background. Appliqué and quilt with pastel embroidery floss to capture a special glow.

Materials

Dimensions given are for prewashed wool pieces. Refer to "All About Wool," beginning on page 5, for selecting and dyeing wool before starting this project. The fabric measurements indicate minimum amounts required for all pieces except the background. Cotton yardage is based on 44"-wide fabric.

10½" x 14½" rectangle for background
10" x 14" rectangle for trunk and branches
Assorted scraps for fruit, birds, and moon
½ yd. coordinating cotton for backing and binding
10½" x 14½" rectangle of lightweight batting
Coordinating embroidery floss or perle cotton

Cutting and Assembly

Note: When working with narrow strips of wool, make sure each piece is cut on the straight of grain. The straight of grain is easy to find; just tear the wool. Trim the frayed edge and use the new straight edge as a reference to cut the strips.

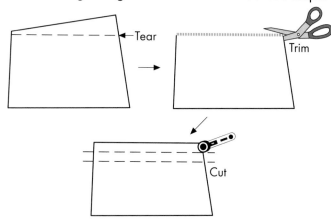

1. Cut the tree trunk and branch fabric into $\frac{3}{8}$"-wide strips. Cut tree trunk 13" long.
2. Cut branches to the following lengths, then cut each end at an angle as shown.

Branch	Dimensions
1	1"
2	$1\frac{3}{4}$"
3	$2\frac{1}{4}$"
4	$2\frac{3}{4}$"
5	$3\frac{1}{2}$"
6	$4\frac{1}{4}$"
7	$4\frac{3}{4}$"
8	$5\frac{1}{2}$"
9	6"
10	$6\frac{1}{2}$"
11	$7\frac{1}{2}$"

3. Pin the tree trunk in place, then the branches, with the longest branch at the bottom and the shortest branch at the top. Appliqué.
4. Pin and appliqué the fruit and birds, then the moon.

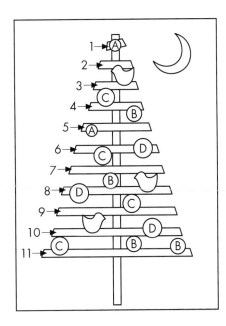

5. Embroider each bird's eye with a French knot.
6. Using the embroidery stitches of your choice, initial and date the front of your quilt. (See "Initialing Your Work" on page 15.)

Finishing the Quilt

Refer to the directions given for finishing the quilt on pages 15–18.

1. Layer the quilt top with batting and backing. Pin or baste the 3 layers together.
2. Quilt the rays of the moonlight, using embroidery floss or perle cotton. Choose quilting thread that is similar to the color of your moon, or use a metallic thread to give a soft glimmer to your quilt.

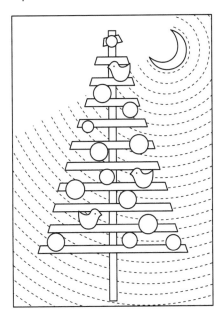

3. Press the back of the quilt, placing a damp cloth between the quilt and the iron.
4. Square up the quilt.
5. Bind the edges.
6. Give the back side of the quilt one final steam pressing.

FLORAL SAMPLER

Finished Quilt Size: 12¾" x 16¼"
Color photo on page 42.

This design evolved from a hooked rug that I designed to give new rug hookers a chance to work with various types of dyed wool. (See the "Floral Sampler" hooked rug on page 55.) Spot-dyed wool, used in several of the flowers, provides a wonderful effect.

Materials

Dimensions given are for prewashed wool pieces. Refer to "All About Wool," beginning on page 5, for selecting and dyeing wool before starting this project. The fabric measurements indicate minimum amounts required for all pieces except the background. Cotton yardage is based on 44"-wide fabric.

12¾" x 16¼" rectangle for background
10" x 13" rectangle for vine
6" x 6" squares of 4 or 5 assorted colors for
    flowers, vase, and dots
½ yd. of coordinating cotton for backing and
    binding
13¼" x 16¾" rectangle of lightweight batting
Coordinating embroidery floss or perle cotton

Cutting and Assembly

1. Using the templates on page 85 and the pullout pattern, trace the patterns and prepare the pieces for appliqué. (See "Wool Appliqué and Quilting Techniques" on pages 13–15.)

Note: I strongly recommend cutting out a lightweight interfacing pattern of the vine before cutting the vine from the wool. (See "Transferring Patterns" on pages 13–14.) I find sequin pins helpful when pinning the pattern to the interfacing and when pinning the prepared piece to the background. Cut the other pieces from interfacing patterns, too, or use tracing paper for the patterns.

2. Pin prepared wool pieces to the background fabric, referring to the quilt diagram below for placement.

3. Using the blanket stitch, appliqué all of the pieces in the order given or in the order of your choice.
4. Embroider details on flowers with chain stitches. Embroider stars on the background, referring to the photo on page 42 for placement. (See "Stitching" on page 14.)
5. Using the embroidery stitches of your choice, initial and date the front of your quilt. (See "Initialing Your Work" on page 15.)

Finishing the Quilt

Refer to the directions given for finishing the quilt on pages 15–18.

1. Layer the quilt top with batting and backing. Pin or baste the 3 layers together.
2. Echo-quilt around the flowers and the stem, or as desired.

Note: To echo-quilt, begin a line of quilting on the background ¼" (or a distance of your choice) from each piece in the design. Quilt the next line of stitches ¼" (or more) from the first line of stitches. Continue quilting in this manner until the entire background is covered. When two lines of quilting meet and create an enclosed space, quilt concentric lines inside the space until it is filled.

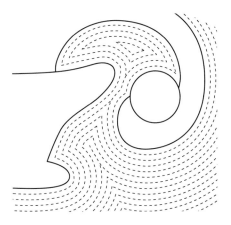

3. Press the back of the quilt, placing a damp cloth between the quilt and the iron.
4. Square up the quilt.
5. Bind the edges.
6. Give the back side of the quilt one final steam pressing.

Folksy Tree Skirt

Finished Quilt Size: 27"-diameter circle
Color photos on pages 48–49.

The images of old-world folk art, whether in embroidery, costume, art, or architecture, have always fascinated and influenced me. Make this as a tree skirt to use for the holidays or make it into a circular wall quilt and enjoy it the year around. Embellish the sweet and rather whimsical folk images in any number of ways.

Materials

Dimensions given are for prewashed wool pieces. Refer to "All About Wool," beginning on page 5, for selecting and dyeing wool before starting this project. The fabric measurements indicate minimum amounts required for all pieces except the background. Cotton yardage is based on 44"-wide fabric.

27" x 27" square for background
10" x 10" squares of 5 or more assorted colors for figures and borders
1 yd. coordinating cotton for backing
⅓ yd. cotton for binding (I used an 18" x 22" "fat quarter.")
29" x 29" square of lightweight batting
Coordinating embroidery floss or perle cotton
3 yds. each of perle cotton in 3 coordinating colors for button loops*
5 buttons, each ⅝" diameter*

*For tree skirt only

Pattern Preparation

1. Cut a paper circle pattern, 27" in diameter, for the tree skirt. My "super-easy circle maker" works likes this: A 27"-diameter circle has a radius of 13½". Cut a strip of cardboard approximately 2" wide and the length of the radius plus 2½", or 16". Draw a line ½" from one of the long edges of the cardboard strip as shown.

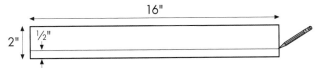

2. On this line, mark a point ½" from the end of the cardboard strip to mark the pivot point. Make another mark on the line, 13½" from the pivot point, then cut a notch with the point placed on the line. The point of a pencil or pen, inserted in the notch at the point, will touch the line at the mark.

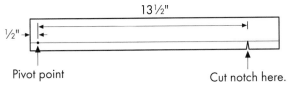

Pivot point   Cut notch here.

3. Spread out and tape together 2 newspaper pages and mark the approximate center. Push a pin through the pivot point of the cardboard and the center of the newspaper, and with a pencil point placed in the notch, push the cardboard strip around to draw the circle. Cut out the circle pattern along the drawn line.

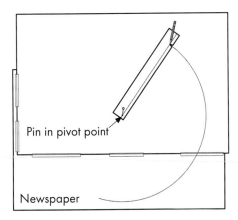

Pin in pivot point

Newspaper

Note: The pivot point and the pencil point must be the same distance from the long edge of the cardboard strip. In this case, that distance is ½".

Tip

Divide the diameter of the circle you are using in half to find the length of the radius.

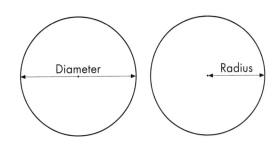

Diameter   Radius

Cutting

1. **CIRCLE:** Pin the newspaper pattern to the wool square and cut out the background circle. Transfer the center point from the pattern to the wool.

2. For the tree skirt, draw a line from the center to the outer edge. (This is the line you will cut along later to make the tree skirt.) Try to place the line on the straight of grain (the same direction as one set of threads in the woven fabric) as shown.

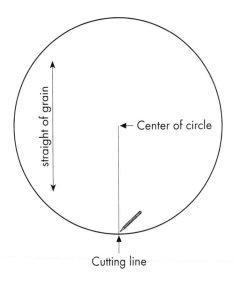

straight of grain

← Center of circle

Cutting line

3. Baste along the cutting line and baste 2 more lines ¼" to each side of the cutting line to mark where the binding will be sewn. These lines will keep you from placing appliqué pieces too near the binding, where they might be too bulky or visually "busy."

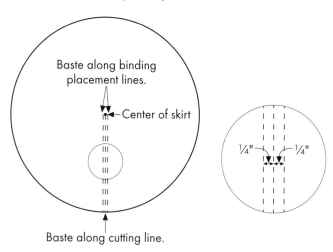

Baste along binding placement lines.

Center of skirt

¼"   ¼"

Baste along cutting line.

4. **BORDER DOTS:** Cut ¾"-wide strips of wool. Cut across the strips to make 1"-long pieces. Now round off the corners of each little ¾" x 1" rectangle to make free-form dots. To keep the folksy nature of the design, do not make the dots identical in shape and size.

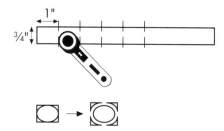

1"

¾"

Note: Later, when you arrange the dots on the background, you may find it necessary to make some of the dots smaller in order to complete a color repeat or to comfortably fill the space.

5. **SCALLOPED EDGE:** Cut 1"-wide strips of wool for the scallops. You will need a row of scallops approximately 85" long, depending on how close to the edge of the tree skirt you place them.

Note: Cutting the scallops from straight strips of fabric is a much better use of fabric; the wool will conform to any size curve you are using. The strips can be any length you are comfortable working with (or the length of the fabric you are using).

6. From these strips, cut the scallops freehand, or use the pattern on page 86. Cut one end of the strip to include a narrow "connector," and cut the other end without it.

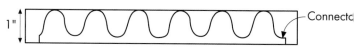

1"

Connecto

Note: The narrow connector slips under the end of the next strip, where there is no connector.

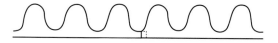

7. Position the scallops and border dots around the edge of the quilt but do not appliqué yet. When you are ready to close the circle, custom-cut a few of the scallops if necessary, making them fatter or smaller to fit your space. For the tree skirt, add connectors to the ends that extend into the binding area.

Binding placement lines

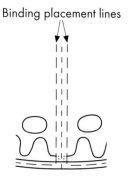

Assembly

1. Using the templates on pages 86–87 and the pullout pattern, trace the remaining patterns and prepare the pieces for appliqué. (See "Wool Appliqué and Quilting Techniques" on pages 13–15.)
2. Appliqué the scalloped edge and border dots, starting with the ends lying to each side of the basted cutting line. Do not extend the dots into the basted area.

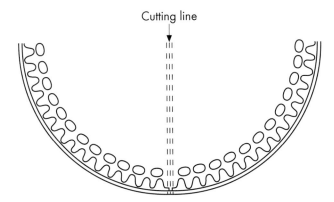

3. Place the quilt's center flower on the background, matching center points.

4. Pin the remaining prepared wool pieces to the background fabric, referring to the quilt diagram on page 36 for placement. When you are pleased with the layout, baste the pieces in place. Usually, for smaller quilts, I just pin the design elements in place, but there are so many pieces that basting is well worth the time and effort.
5. Appliqué the pieces, using the blanket stitch. (See "Stitching" on page 14.)
6. Embroider details, referring to the stitch recommendations on the templates, or use your own. Fill the area between the scalloped and dot borders with a chain stitch/lazy-daisy variation as shown.

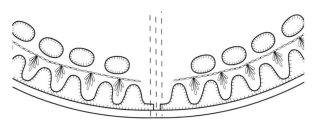

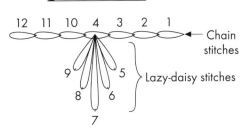

7. Using the embroidery stitches of your choice, initial and date the front of your quilt. (See "Initialing Your Work" on page 15.)

Finishing the Quilt

*Refer to the directions given for
finishing the quilt on pages 15–18.*

1. Layer the quilt top with batting and backing.
   Pin or baste the 3 layers together.
2. Quilt as desired in multicolored perle cotton or
   embroidery floss around the central figures and
   even on the figures themselves if you like.
   *Make sure none of your quilting stitches run
   through the basted area, or you'll cut the
   quilting when you cut the tree skirt opening.*
3. Press the back of the quilt, placing a damp
   cloth between the quilt and the iron.
4. Cut the opening along the cutting line.

5. Bind the edges, using 1¼"-wide, bias-cut
   binding strips.
6. Position the first button loop at the lower edge.
   Arrange and baste 4 more loops, each 2"
   apart, along the left edge of the opening.
   Make the button-loop cord by braiding together 3 colors of perle cotton. Sew the braid
   in place, tucking the ends of the cord under the
   center flower and the border dot as shown.
   Sew the buttons to the quilt.

Tuck end of
braid under.

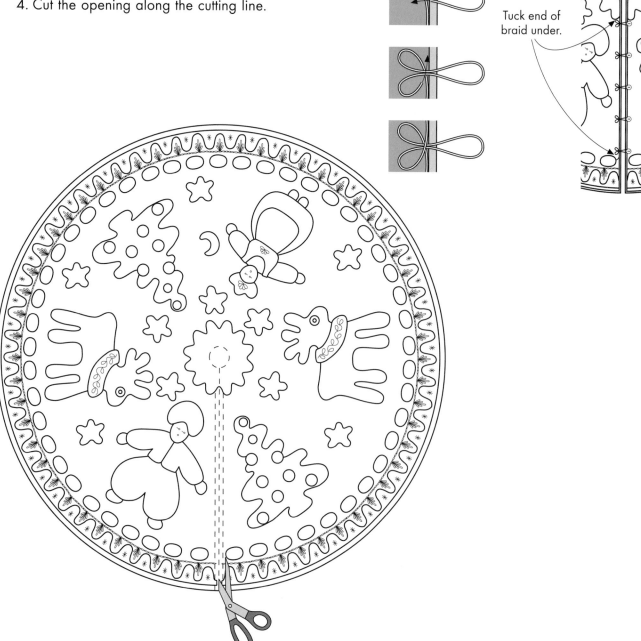

Gallery

Rise and Shine *by Janet Carija Brandt, 1994, Indianapolis, Indiana, 17¹/₂" x 21¹/₂". An Art Deco-inspired design shows off the dip-dyed wool rays to great effect.*

Flowers and Hearts by Janet Carija Brandt, 1994, Indianapolis, Indiana, 10" x 13". The navy blue and pink color scheme is accented with bright yellow flowers. (Collection of Joyce Freeman)

Floral Sampler by Janet Carija Brandt, 1994, Indianapolis, Indiana, 12³/4" x 16¹/4". A flowing vinelike stem has a variety of blooms and buds. Some of the flowers are spot-dyed wool. (Collection of Virginia Carija)

Flowers and Hearts by Janet Carija Brandt, 1993, Indianapolis, Indiana, 10" x 13 1/2". Flowers surround the hearts in hands, all done in hand-dyed pastels.

Flowers and Hearts by Janet Carija Brandt, 1993, Indianapolis, Indiana, 10" x 13". The traditional heart-in-hand folk motif is rendered in hand-dyed, recycled wool.

Pink Bird by Janet Carija Brandt, 1994, Indianapolis, Indiana, 13¼" x 20¾". A pink bird living in a two-story home is the subject of this whimsical design.

Yellow Bird by Debra Haggard, 1994, Indianapolis, Indiana, 13½" x 21". This all-cotton appliqué quilt is an interpretation of the Pink Bird design.

Moonlight Tree by Lois Trout, 1994, Indianapolis, Indiana, 10" x 14". Lois very thoughtfully appliquéd the tree branches that catch the moonlight in a brighter color than those limbs in the shadows. Very effective!

Moonlight Tree by Janet Carija Brandt, 1994, Indianapolis, Indiana, 10" x 14". Multicolored fruits and little bluebirds nestle in this tree on a moonlit night.

Lady Liberty by Debra Haggard, 1994, Indianapolis, Indiana, 10" x 14". Lady Liberty's underskirt is covered with embroidered stars, and her sky is filled with appliquéd stars.

Uncle Sam by Debra Haggard, 1994, Indianapolis, Indiana, 10" x 14". Uncle Sam's flag has wool appliquéd stripes, and the background has golden appliquéd stars.

Lady Liberty by Janet Carija Brandt, 1994, Indianapolis, Indiana, 10" x 14". Lady Liberty has a flowing gown and a golden crown.

Uncle Sam by Janet Carija Brandt, 1994, Indianapolis, Indiana, 10" x 14". Uncle Sam proudly carries the American flag in front of a star-quilted background.

Folksy Tree Skirt by Janet Carija Brandt, 1994, Indianapolis, Indiana, 27" diameter. An old-world costumed boy and girl, two trees, two reindeer, and a colorful border wrap around this tree skirt in bright hand-dyed wool.

Folksy Tree Quilt by Debby Eads, 1994, Indianapolis, Indiana, 25" diameter. Homespun colors add to the charm and beauty of this quilt.

40 Days and 40 Nights
by Janet Carija Brandt, 1994, Indianapolis, Indiana, 17¹/₂" x 24". Noah's animals come in shades of pink, orange, and rust for this voyage. (Collection of Claudia Peresman)

40 Days and 40 Nights *by Janet Carija Brandt, 1994, Indianapolis, Indiana, 17¹/₂" x 24". Recycled wool in plaids, checks, and solids were overdyed for this nursery-room favorite done in grays, reds, and black.*

50   Gallery

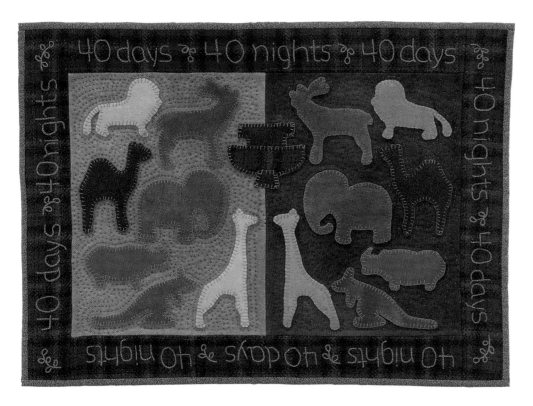

40 Days and 40 Nights
by Norma Crabiel, 1994,
Indianapolis, Indiana,
17½" x 24". The plaid
border ties all the colors
together and provides an
easy guide for embroider-
ing the letters.

Two Pink Birds by Janet Carija Brandt, 1994,
Indianapolis, Indiana, 13" x 17". This variation of
the Pink Bird quilt features the Pink Bird and her
twin sister with their matching condos and moons.

Floral Salad by Janet Carija Brandt, 1994,
Indianapolis, Indiana, 13½" x 16". All the little
bits and pieces of this WOW! quilt reminded me
of a fruit and flower salad, gently tossed.

Gallery **51**

Petal Hearts by Debra Haggard, 1994, Indianapolis, Indiana, 32" x 32". A dark and dramatic plaid was the inspiration for this color scheme. Here the centers of the hearts are tied in place, and the background fabric was allowed to extend beyond the edges of the hearts.

Modern Mini Penny Rug by Janet Carija Brandt, 1994, Indianapolis, Indiana, 9³/₄" x 12³/₄". Traditional penny rugs were made of uniform pieces of wool in a symmetrical layout. Look what happens when color and placement explodes!

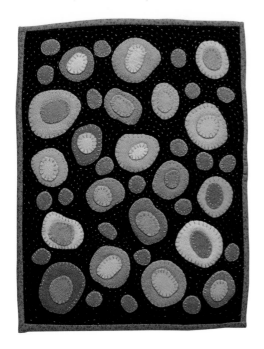

Silhouettes by Janet Carija Brandt, 1994, Indianapolis, Indiana, 14" x 17". A color combination often seen in traditional woven coverlets, this WOW! quilt boldly showcases many folk-art shapes.

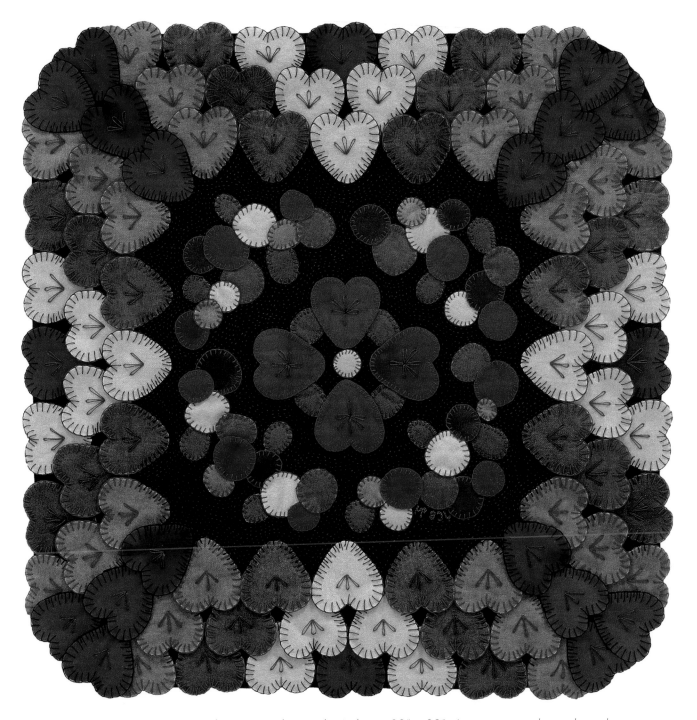

Petal Hearts by Janet Carija Brandt, 1994, Indianapolis, Indiana, 32" x 32". A variation on the traditional penny rug, this quilt is made of hearts that appear as petals when the top half of each heart is left to hang free from the foundation.

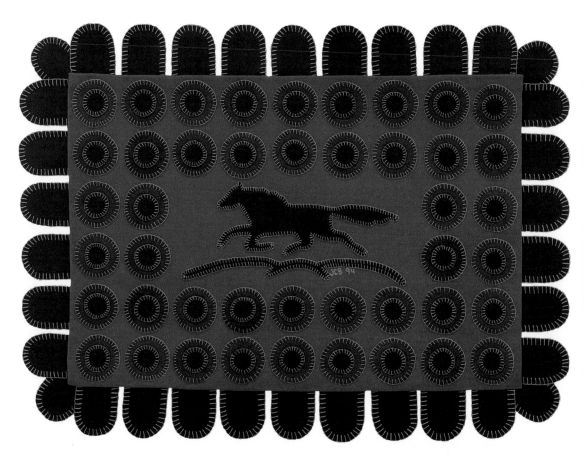

Running Horse by Janet Carija Brandt, 1994, Indianapolis, Indiana, 30$\frac{1}{2}$" x 22$\frac{1}{2}$". This traditional penny rug features a running horse at the center and a tongue border around the outside.

Miss Freedom by Janet Carija Brandt, 1990, Indianapolis, Indiana, 6" x 11$\frac{1}{2}$". This small hooked rug is based on a famous piece of folk art.

Stars and Stripes by Janet Carija Brandt, 1993, Indianapolis, Indiana, 10" x 13$\frac{1}{4}$". This WOW! quilt, inspired by the "Miss Freedom" hooked rug at left, makes a stunning wall hanging.

Hearts and Hands by Janet Carija Brandt, 1988, Indianapolis, Indiana, 22" x 22". The first rug I designed and hooked shows the three different backgrounds I used—because I kept running out of wool!

Floral Sampler by Janet Carija Brandt, 1994, Indianapolis, Indiana, 7" x 10¼". The inspiration for the WOW! Floral Sampler on page 42, this hooking project features flowers of dip-dyed, spot-dyed, and gradation-dyed wools.

Pink Bird by Janet Carija Brandt, 1994, Indianapolis, Indiana, 9" x 11½". This small hooked rug was the original Pink Bird design.

Red Hen Rug by Janet Carija Brandt, 1994, Indianapolis, Indiana, 22" x 27". Only recycled wool was used in this rug to prove that hooking materials are readily available everywhere.

Petal Rugs

Petal, tongue, or scalloped rugs come from the same family of Early-American rugs that includes penny rugs. Penny rugs represent another example of Yankee ingenuity and making do with materials that are on hand. Traditional petal rugs do not have a batting layer and are not quilted, but they usually do have a cotton or linen backing.

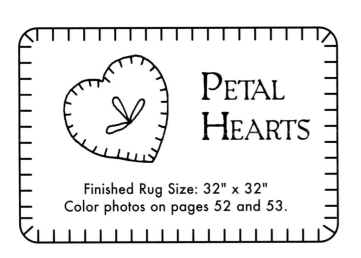

PETAL HEARTS

Finished Rug Size: 32" x 32"
Color photos on pages 52 and 53.

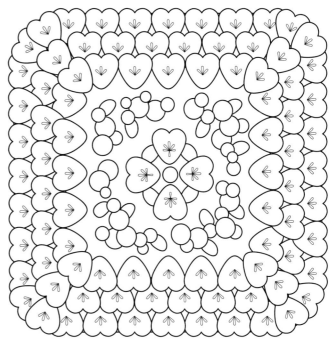

For this petal rug, I added a batting layer and quilted it, making this a warm and cozy lap robe, table topper, or wall hanging.

Materials

Dimensions given are for prewashed wool pieces. Refer to "All About Wool," beginning on page 5, for selecting and dyeing wool before starting this project. The fabric measurements indicate minimum amounts required for all pieces except the background. Cotton yardage is based on 44"-wide fabric.

32" x 32" square for background
15" x 20" rectangles of cream, green, tan, and cranberry for hearts
10" x 10" squares of cream, green, tan, brown, rose, and cranberry for flowers and leaves
1 yd. cotton for backing
½ yd. cotton for bias binding
34" x 34" square of lightweight batting
Coordinating or contrasting perle cotton

Cutting

1. Using the templates on the pullout pattern and referring to the cutting chart below, trace the patterns and prepare the pieces for appliqué. (See "Wool Appliqué and Quilting Techniques" on pages 13–15.)
2. Cut the following numbers of hearts, flowers, and leaves for each color, or cut pieces from the colors of your choice. I cut each small, medium, and large flower a slightly different size to add to the folksy randomness of the design.

Assembly

1. Using a strand of perle cotton, work the blanket stitch around all of the hearts except the 4 cranberry hearts that go in the center of the quilt. (See "Stitching" on page 14.) I try to cut the perle cotton long enough to go all the way around a heart without having to change thread. For me, about 40" is just right, but the size and closeness of your stitches will determine what is right for you. As you work, leave space between the stitches for a second row of stitches that you'll use to attach the heart to the background. (See step 6 on page 59.)

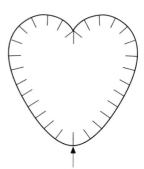

Begin and end here.

Note: Begin and end the row of blanket stitches at the point of the heart so that no knots show on the floppy top "petals" of the heart pieces.

Piece	Cream	Green	Tan	Brown	Rose	Cranberry
Hearts	20	24	24	–	–	24
Large Flowers	5	–	5	1	3	5
Med. Flowers	3	–	3	7	5	
Small Flowers	1	–	1	–	–	
Leaves	–	15	–	–	–	–

2. With chalk, pins, or basting thread, mark the center lines on the background. Measure and mark 7½" from the outer edge along each line and place the "point" of one cream heart at each of these marks.

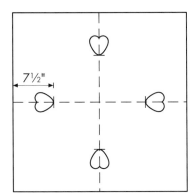

3. Working from the center heart out, add the other hearts in the first row. Use a yardstick to check the straightness of the row and to check the distances between hearts as you place them. Place the hearts so that they just touch at their widest point. Each corner heart overlaps the heart on each side. Pin each heart in the first row with just one pin near the point.

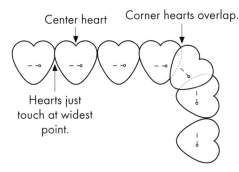

Center heart

Corner hearts overlap.

Hearts just touch at widest point.

Note: This is one time I do not recommend using sequin pins. You may be doing quite a bit of adjusting as you work, and longer straight pins are easier to grab and move.

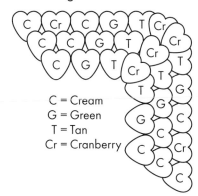

C = Cream
G = Green
T = Tan
Cr = Cranberry

4. Refering to the illustration below left for color placement, pin the next row of hearts so that the point of each heart lies under the first row at the point where 2 hearts touch. Repeat for the third row. It's OK if the tops of the third row's hearts hang over the edge of the background.

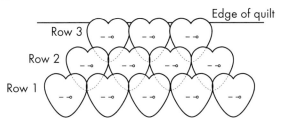

Edge of quilt

Row 3
Row 2
Row 1

5. At the outer corner, overlap 2 hearts of the same color as shown.

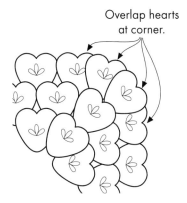

Overlap hearts at corner.

Note: Be prepared to play around with the placement of the hearts. It isn't an exact kind of design, which of course is the charm of all folk art.

6. Using the blanket stitch, appliqué the hearts to the background. Work the new stitches between the first set of stitches, attaching only the bottom half of the heart to the background. Pin back the tops of the overlapping hearts as you work.

Attach heart to background with these stitches.

7. With contrasting perle cotton, work large lazy-daisy stitches in all of the hearts as shown. (See "Stitching" on page 14.)

8. Arrange the center hearts, flowers, and leaves, following the diagram below or choosing your own pleasing arrangement. When you are satisfied with the design, pin, then appliqué, using the blanket stitch.

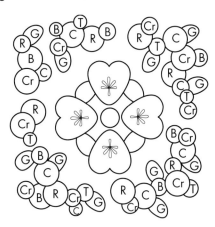

C = Cream
G = Green
T = Tan
B = Brown
R = Rose
Cr = Cranberry

9. Embroider the center hearts with a lazy-daisy stitch as shown.

10. Using the embroidery stitches of your choice, initial and date the front of your petal rug. (See "Initialing Your Work" on page 15.)

Finishing the Rug

Refer to the directions given for finishing the rug on pages 15–18.

1. Layer the rug top with batting and backing. Pin or baste the 3 layers together.
2. Quilt the center area.
3. Leave the corners square or round them off, using a plate or saucer as a guide. Be sure to fold the "petals" of the hearts away from the cutting line.

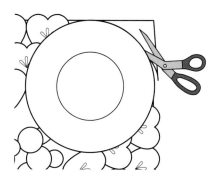

4. Press the back of the rug, placing a damp cloth between the rug and the iron.
5. Bind the edges. If you cut the background to make rounded corners, be sure to use bias-cut binding strips. Either $1/2$"-wide purchased double-fold bias tape or $1\frac{1}{2}$"-wide, bias-cut binding strips can be used.

Penny Rugs

Like so many facets of our textile heritage, penny rugs have their own colorful history. At first, the word "rug" had nothing to do with a floor covering. Instead, "rugg" meant a coarse covering for the bed or table. In the early nineteenth century, textiles were too precious for the heavy wear and tear they would receive on the floor. Hooked bed coverings and appliquéd table mats were our ancestors' early rugs. As a variety of fabrics became more widely available, hooked rugs, then penny rugs found their way to their present-day dual tasks of decoration and utility for the floor.

True penny rugs evolved shortly after the Civil War. Tradition tells us the name comes from one of the objects used as a pattern to cut the many circles needed for the design. Frequently, geometric patterns of early penny rugs *consisted of layers of circles, two, three or four circles high, with each layer a little smaller than the layer under it.* The blanket stitch was used to secure the pennies to each other and to the background.

The choice of background fabric seemed to be a matter of either personal preference or simply whatever was on hand. Linen, wool, or cotton were all used. I use wool on the front side and line the back of the penny rug with cotton.

The Victorian era saw penny rugs more richly embroidered than ever before and introduced "tongue" borders, similar to the one on the Running Horse penny rug on page 62.

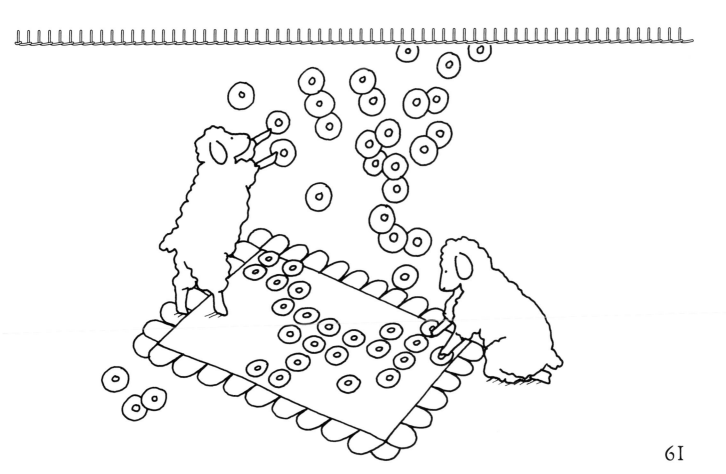

Running Horse

Finished Rug Size: 30½" x 22½"
Color photo on page 54.

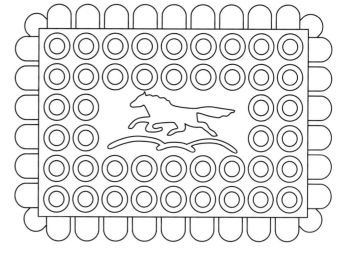

Penny rugs are sometimes completely covered with circles or "pennies." Occasionally, such as in this design, pennies surround a central design.

Materials

Dimensions given are for prewashed wool pieces. Refer to "All About Wool," beginning on page 5, for selecting and dyeing wool before starting this project. The fabric measurements indicate minimum amounts required for all pieces except the background. Cotton yardage is based on 44"-wide fabric.

Note: Fabric amounts are based on the Option 2 method of cutting out pennies. Option 1 may require more fabric.

18" x 26" rectangle of red for background
15" x 20" rectangle of green for large pennies
10" x 16" rectangle of navy blue for small pennies
15" x 20" rectangle of navy blue for "tongues"
7" x 13" rectangle of navy blue for horse and ground line
19" x 27" rectangle of cotton for backing
4 skeins gold embroidery floss

Cutting

1. Using the "tongue" template on the pullout pattern, trace the pattern and cut 34 tongues from the 15" x 20" rectangle of navy blue wool. (See "Wool Appliqué and Quilting Techniques" on pages 13–15.)
2. From the green wool, cut 44 large pennies, and from the 10" x 16" rectangle of navy blue wool, cut 44 small pennies. There are two ways to cut out the circles for your penny rug:

Option 1: This method is for those of you who like precise cutting lines.

1. From lightweight template plastic, trace, then cut out large and small circle templates from the template patterns on the pullout pattern. The plastic template holds up well to repeated use in a design like this better than a paper template.

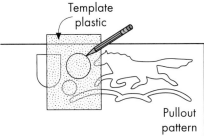

Template plastic

Pullout pattern

2. With a chalk pencil, trace around the pattern onto the wool. The wool fabric loves to stretch and pull, so hold the pattern securely on the wool as you trace.

3. Cut out each wool penny.

Option 2: How comfortable you are with freehand cutting will determine whether this next option is for you.

1. With the rotary cutter and cutting guide, cut 6 strips, each 2½" wide, along the long edge of the green wool. Cut across these strips at 2½" intervals to make 44 squares, each 2½" x 2½", for the large pennies.

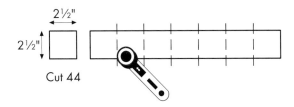

2½"

2½"

Cut 44

2. For the small pennies, cut 5 strips, each 1½" wide, along the long edge of the navy blue wool. Cut across these strips at 1½" intervals to make 1½" x 1½" squares.

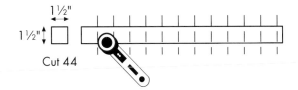

1½"

1½"

Cut 44

3. To make circles, use scissors to round off the corners of each square cut in steps 1 and 2.

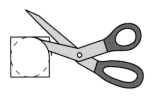

Tip

I check for accuracy and symmetry by comparing each newly cut circle with a master circle pattern or template, such as the pattern in this book. Try to keep the cut edges very smooth. Blanket stitches won't hide ragged edges.

Assembly

1. Stack a small navy blue circle on top of each large green circle. Appliqué the small penny to the large one with the blanket stitch, making sure the small penny is centered on the larger one.

Make 44

2. Arrange the penny stacks on the background, referring to the diagram on page 62. Cut out the horse and ground line and arrange on the rug. (You don't want to appliqué all of the pennies in place only to find you didn't leave enough room for the horse!) Appliqué pennies, horse, and ground line, using the blanket stitch.

3. Turn under the background fabric ½" toward the back side of the rug, mitering at the corners. Press, always pressing on the back side and placing a damp cloth between the wool and the iron.

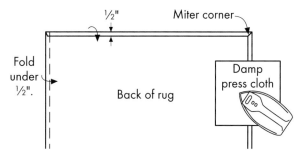

4. Use a blanket stitch around the long rounded edge of the tongue pieces.

5. On the back side of the rug, arrange and pin or baste the tongues around the folded edge of the rug. Do not add the 4 corner tongues yet. Overlap the unstitched edge of each tongue about ½", so it is even with the edge of the hem.

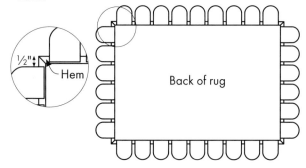

6. Turn the rug over to the front and slipstitch the tongues in place, where they join the rug.

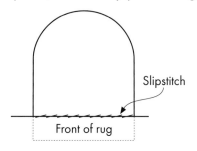

7. Position each of the 4 remaining tongues diagonally at each corner. Stitch in place along the back side, being careful not to stitch through to the front.

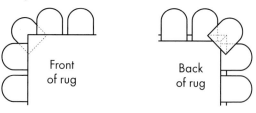

8. Using the embroidery stitches of your choice, initial and date the front of your rug. Turn the rug over and press from the back.

9. With the rug placed flat, wrong side up, lay the cotton backing, right side up, over the back of the rug. Pin-baste, making sure to smooth out the backing carefully from the center of the rug to the outside.

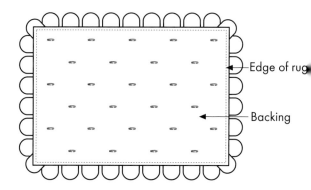

10. Fold under the edge of the backing to meet the folded edge of the front of the rug. Slipstitch in place, then give it a final pressing.

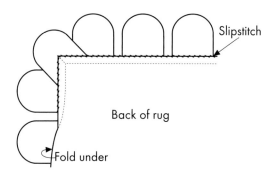

Traditional Hooked Rugs

Rug hooking, like quilting, is a recycler's dream come true. This all-American craft became popular in the mid-1800s, when burlap, the fabric most commonly used for the foundation, became more readily available. Cast-off burlap feed sacks became the framework for rugs that featured designs of the family home, its occupants, pets, and garden. Subject matter also included wild and whimsical geometric and abstract designs. Any fabric on hand might find its way into the top of the rug, including Dad's old military uniform, Aunt Edna's mourning gown, and Jimmy's red flannel long johns! Women drew their own designs or purchased patterns from peddlers passing through town.

Like so many crafts, rug hooking has passed in and out of style over the years. Happily, it enjoys an ever-growing renaissance today.

ESTIMATING WOOL YARDAGE

Some books list fabric amounts in weight, but I find that method difficult to follow. Amounts given in most patterns are approximate. Depending on the width of your strips, the height of your loops, and how closely you pack your loops, you may require different amounts of wool than those specified in the pattern.

When I made the Red Hen Rug on page 72, I kept track of how much wool I used so that I could share it with you. When you try a project of your own design or a pattern where yardage amounts are not included, follow this rule of thumb: multiply the area you plan to cover with wool by 5 to find the amount of wool you need. For example, if the pattern has a small house about 3" wide and 2" high, the total area to cover is 6 square inches. So, you will need 5 times that number, or a total of 30 square inches of wool to hook the house.

Although the wool requirements for the Red Hen rug are given in square inches, keep in mind that in rug hooking any size piece of wool is usable. If you need 500 square inches of green, that could be 1 rectangle, measuring 20" x 25"; 20 squares, each measuring 5" x 5"; or 1 strip, measuring 2" x 250"! Each way, you have 500 square inches, and all of the wool can be put to good use.

Color placement also affects the amount of wool needed. If, for example, you choose to use a different color than the pattern recommends, you must make adjustments based on the calculations given above.

Note: If you follow the random dyeing method I described on pages 10–11, obtaining plenty of color choices in sufficient quantities for making the Red Hen rug won't pose a problem.

Of course, not all of the design elements of a rug come in easy-to-measure rectangular shapes, so a great deal of "guesstimation" must occur. But take heart! Some of the most successful rugs are created by running out of a specific color of wool and not being able to match it with a new supply. Necessity is certainly the mother of invention at moments like those.

2" x 3" = 6 sq. in.
6 sq. in. x 5 = 30 sq. in.

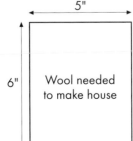

Wool needed to make house

One way to disguise an unplanned color change is to introduce a new color slowly, mixing the old and new colors and gradually changing to the new color.

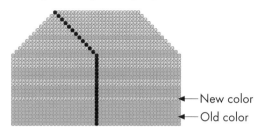

New color ←
Old color ←

Another trick is to alter the design, adding an inner border or another design element. In my very first rug, I ran out of the original background color after only the center portion was hooked. I introduced a ribbon-like border around that area and started a new color outside of it. Then I ran out of that color, too! Next, I added a wreathlike border of flowers and started my third background. By then, I was taking no chances, so I made the final border a two-tone stripe. The results were unexpected, but it is still one of my favorite hooked pieces. (See "Hearts and Hands" on page 55.)

FOUNDATION FABRICS

The foundation fabric you use for your rug is just as important as the wool you hook into it. The easiest fabric to learn on and the most readily available is burlap. Burlap's stiffness makes it easier for a beginner to catch on to the rhythm of hooking and makes it harder to overpack loops (pulling too many loops through the fabric), which makes a rug wavy and lumpy. Look for even-weave Scottish burlap, which is specially woven for rug hooking. Don't be tempted to try the weak and irregular all-purpose burlap at your local craft shop. I can relate countless tales of woe about weak foundation fabrics falling apart, sometimes before the rug is completely hooked. As in quilting, the cost of the fabric you invest in a project is small compared to your time. Strive to work with the best fabric you can.

After their first rug, most rug hookers have a feel for the basic rug-hooking techniques. For the next rugs, I recommend using 100% cotton monk's cloth or linen as a foundation fabric. Monk's cloth is my favorite. It is soft to the touch, and it is easy to pull loops through the fabric. Its only disadvantage is that it is also easy to overpack. (This problem is easily solved by simply removing some of the loops in the lumpy areas.)

Linen foundation fabric looks like and is as easy to use as burlap. It is twice the price of burlap but still a bargain when you consider the time you will invest. One drawback of linen is that the linen fibers sometimes migrate or "beard" to the top of the rug, just as some battings do on quilts. In a light-colored rug, this is not noticeable, but it is annoying against a dark background.

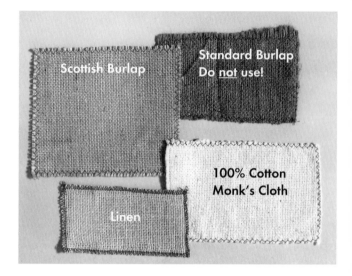

As you can see from these pros and cons, the right foundation fabric for you is the fabric that you find easy to work with and provides the desired results. For their patterns, most designers give you the choice of your favorite foundation fabric.

Note: If you decide to draw your own pattern, be sure to use a permanent marking pen.

TOOLS

As with all crafts, rug hooking has a few basic tools that make the job easier.

Hooking Frame: You can get by with using an embroidery hoop or by pinning the hooking pattern to a padded picture frame. Both are excellent options for a person with three hands! For the rest of us, starting with a quilting hoop on a floor stand works well. The stand eliminates the need for the third hand.

The best option by far is a frame designed for rug hooking. The Puritan frame has been around for many years and will last and last and last. (I have one that I purchased nine years ago and I also have the one my Gramma purchased over thirty years ago, and the two frames look identical!)

This frame comes with two adjustable sides for tightening the foundation fabric on the frame. You can also purchase a floor stand to hold this frame.

Some people insist that the frame be used on a tabletop or a stand. I prefer to hold the frame in my lap, which is probably why I like the lightweight and affordable Appleton frame best of all. It does not have adjustable sides, but I have no trouble keeping the monk's cloth stretched tight.

Both the Appleton and Puritan frames are constructed with four strips of metal needle boards, carding strips, or metal Velcro®, which rug hookers call gripper strips. They are short and prickly and work like a dream.

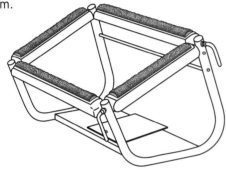

One type of hooking frame

HOOK: The hook most commonly used for making rugs looks like a crochet hook with a fat wooden handle. I work with the most comfortable hook I own, the one my Gramma gave to me nine years ago. Since it is the most inexpensive piece of rug-hooking equipment you'll need, I suggest purchasing the hook that fits your hand and hooking style the best.

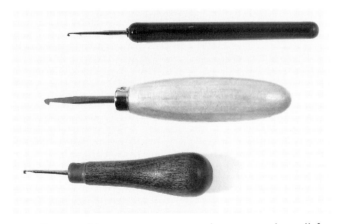

CUTTER: Alas, rotary cutters do not work well for cutting wool strips. The wool scoots around under the cutting guide too much to get a straight, narrow strip time after time.

It is possible to cut all of the wool strips by hand with scissors, but it is time-consuming and only worth

the effort if you want the look of a highly primitive type of rug. There are three commercial cutters available today. The Bliss, Rigby, and Fraser cutters are all excellent machines and very similar in price. The Bliss model attaches to the tabletop with suction cups. The Rigby and Fraser machines are similar to each other, and each machine clamps to the tabletop. (See page 88 for information on where to order cutters and other rug-hooking equipment.)

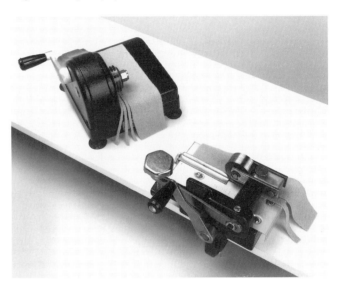

Rug-Hooking Techniques

Cutting Strips

Cutters for rug hooking come with interchangeable cutting heads that cut strips of wool from $3/32$" wide (#3 cut) to $1/4$" (#8 cut) or wider.

Cut Number	Cut Strip Width
3	$3/32$"
4	$1/8$"
5	$5/32$"
6	$3/16$"
8	$1/4$"

The width of the wool strips greatly affects the look of the rug. The narrower the cut, the more loops you must make. This way, you can achieve more detail. Depending on the weave of your foundation fabric, narrow strips (such as a #3 cut) may require that you make a loop in almost every space in the foundation fabric. Wider strips require skipping more spaces.

Before cutting strips, tear the wool into 3"- or 4"-wide strips. It is much easier to feed this size strip through the cutter than to wrestle with a wider piece. Use any length that you find comfortable.

Tearing the wool instead of cutting it serves an important purpose. The torn edge gives a straight edge that follows along the long threads in the fabric, giving it greater strength when it is cut into strips. If the wool is not cut on the straight edge of the fabric, it will fall apart with a gentle tug when it is cut into a narrow strip.

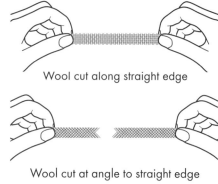

Wool cut along straight edge

Wool cut at angle to straight edge

If you know which way the lengthwise grain of the wool runs on your piece of fabric, it is preferable to cut along it, rather than across it. If you aren't sure, either direction will probably be all right. Cut two test strips and pull gently on them to see if there is a difference in strength.

When cutting plaids and stripes, you have a choice. If you cut along the "stripes" of the pattern, you will get solid strips of different colors. If you cut across the pattern, you will get multicolored strips. Hook a small sample swatch of each to see the varied results you can get from one piece of wool.

Develop the habit of reversing the direction and flipping your wool as you run it through the cutter to make successive cuts. The end that went through the cutter last should be turned over (top side on the bottom) and fed through the cutter first for the next cut.

Organizing Wool Strips

Keep your wool strips organized by using one or more of the following methods. In addition to keeping colors separated, these methods are helpful for keeping different shades of one color in order.

Method 1: Make deep accordion folds in stiff paper. Place a different color or shade in each section. To store the strips, fold up and secure with ribbon or a rubber band.

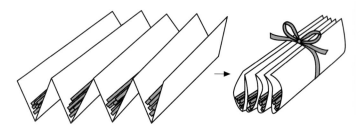

Method 2: Keep colors sorted by placing bunches of strips in pages of magazines or catalogs.

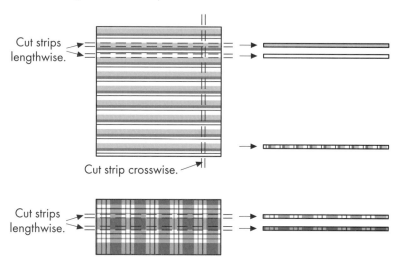

Cut strips lengthwise.

Cut strip crosswise.

Cut strips lengthwise.

Method 3: Sew a ribbon or fabric tape to a dish towel or fasten with safety pins. Tuck the strips in the openings. Roll and tie to store.

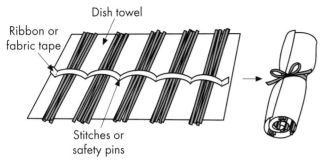

Ribbon or fabric tape

Dish towel

Stitches or safety pins

Hooking the Rug

1. If you are using your own design, place the foundation fabric over the pattern and trace the design onto the foundation fabric, using a permanent marking pen.

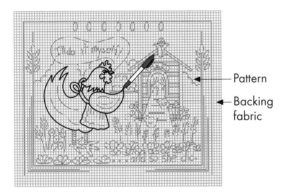

Pattern

Backing fabric

2. To prevent fraying, secure the edges of the foundation fabric with zigzag stitches, several rows of straight stitches, or masking tape.

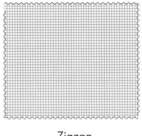

Zigzag

Fold over.

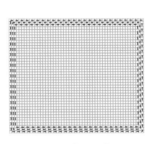 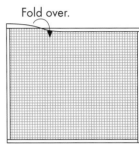

Straight stitches   Masking tape

3. With the design side up, place the foundation fabric in the quilting hoop or on the hooking frame. If you are hooking on burlap, the fabric only needs to be snug in the frame or hoop. When working with monk's cloth, keep your fabric very taut to avoid overcrowding or overpacking the loops.

Tip

I use a light table when I transfer my designs. If you do not have one, you can make one by setting a piece of glass or transparent plastic between two tables (or remove a leaf from one table) and putting a lamp underneath.

Tip

If the pattern is not large enough to fill the hoop, sew scraps of any extra fabric to the edges of the foundation fabric to make it large enough to stretch in the hoop.

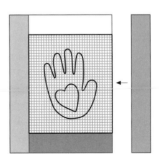

4. I usually start with a center section of the rug. Hold the hook in your right hand. (Reverse instructions if you are left-handed.) Begin by holding the hook like a pencil. As you work, you can try different grips to see what works best for you.

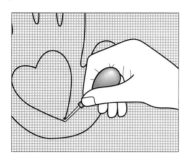

5. Hold a strip of wool fabric in your left hand between the thumb and forefinger under the frame and pattern. Use the hand underneath to guide the wool as it is being pulled up by the hook and to make sure there are no loops on the back of the rug.

6. Insert the hook through the top of the pattern. With the barb of the hook, catch the wool strip underneath and pull the end of the wool out to the top of the pattern, leaving about ½" sticking out.

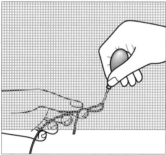

7. Insert the hook in the next hole of your pattern fabric and draw up a loop of wool.

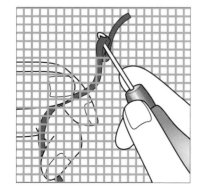

Tip

Generally, make each loop as high as the wool is wide.

8. Continue in this manner, trying to make each loop the same height. Do not try to make a loop in every single hole. You can skip every fourth or fifth hole. If you pack the loops too closely, the rug will get lumpy. If they are hooked too loosely, you will see "holidays" of foundation fabric peeking through. Practice will eventually show you the just-right spacing between the loops.

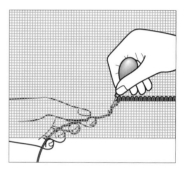

9. When you come to the end of a wool strip, pull the tail end to the top side. Pull the end of the new strip up through that same hole, once again leaving a little tail, then continue hooking. After a few loops are hooked around the tails, trim the ends even with the tops of the loops.
10. Outline the area to be hooked, then fill in the area with one or more colors as desired.

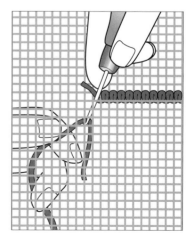

Finishing the Rug

You're almost done! There is only one more process before your new heirloom is complete.

1. Staystitch or zigzag stitch the backing fabric 1" from the finished edge of the hooking. Trim away the excess.

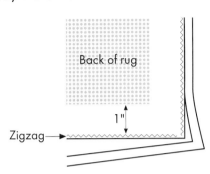

2. Fold the corner of the rug to the back side.

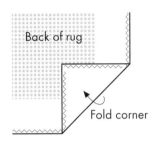

3. Fold each side up to form a mitered corner.

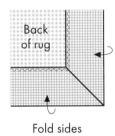

4. Slipstitch the foundation fabric to the back of the rug.

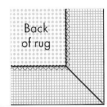

Slipstitch hem to back of rug.

5. Sew rug tape over the hem if desired. Sew one edge of the tape close to the last row of hooking and the other edge to the back of the rug, covering the foundation-fabric hem and mitering the corners.

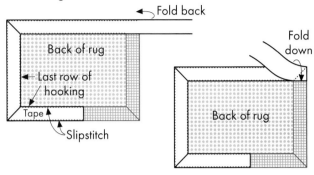

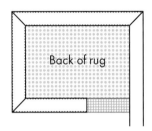

Tips

♥ As you pull up on the new loop, always pull toward the loop you just hooked.

♥ If you need to move a color across an already-hooked area, don't cross wool strips over hooked areas on the back side of your work. When you finish hooking in one area, pull the wool to the top and clip, then begin again in the new area. This keeps the back from becoming lumpy and prevents loops on the back, which are easily caught and pulled out.

♥ Don't try to copy a hooked rug pattern, loop for loop, as you would for counted cross-stitch, needlepoint, or latch-hook patterns. Rug hooking is personal and no two people hook exactly alike.

♥ Do remember to stand up and gently stretch occasionally.

Red Hen Rug

Finished Rug Size: 19³/₄" x 24³/₄"
Color photo on page 56.

"Red" is certainly a "woman of the '90s." She plants, grows, harvests, mills the wheat, and bakes the cake—and takes care of the kids, too! But then, most women have always been working women!

Note: The pattern for this rug produces a slightly smaller rug than the one shown on page 56.

Materials:

See "Estimating Wool Yardage" on pages 65-66. Refer to "All About Wool," beginning on page 5, for selecting and dyeing wool before starting this project. The Cushing Perfection dyes I used to make "Red Hen" were: Bright Green, Purple, Buttercup Yellow, Old Gold, Cherry, Cardinal, and Copenhagen Blue. For each of the colors, I started with a 10" x 14" soaked piece of three different wools.

To make each of the colors in the rug, I used the following recipe:
Greens: ¼ tsp. Bright Green
Yellows: ⅛ tsp. Buttercup Yellow and ⅛ tsp. Old Gold

Reds: ⅛ tsp. Cherry and ⅛ tsp. Cardinal
Purples: ¼ tsp. Purple
Blues: ¼ tsp. Copenhagen Blue

Remember, overdyeing wool with these colors will produce approximations of the colors shown in the photo on page 56. For the sky, I began with various shades of gray wool, which, when overdyed, became an assortment of grayed blues.

500 square inches (20" x 25" total) of assorted greens for vegetation
400 square inches (20" x 20" total) of assorted yellows for chicks and details
1,400 square inches (35" x 40" total) of assorted purples for background

900 square inches (30" x 30" total) of assorted blues for coop and sky

1,350 square inches (30" x 45" total) of assorted reds for hen, details, and border

28" x 33" rectangle of foundation fabric (See "Foundation Fabrics" on page 66.)

3 yds. rug or twill tape for outside edge

Assembly

If this is your first rug-hooking project, I recommend that you hook a few practice rows outside the rug's border. After hooking a couple of rows, up and down, back and forth, you will be ready to start your rug.

There is no exact order in which you must hook the different areas of the rug. I usually start in the middle of a rug and work my way to the edges, first outlining each shape, then filling it in with rows of stitches. It is best to hook tiny details in an area first and then immediately fill in around them to help hold and define their shape. (See directions for the Red Hen's eye in steps 4 and 5.)

1. Using the pullout pattern, trace the pattern onto the foundation fabric. (See "Foundation Fabrics" on page 66.)
2. Prepare wool strips. I hooked the Red Hen rug with $5/32$"-wide strips of wool (#5 cut). (See "Cutting Strips" on pages 67–68.)
3. Start by hooking the outer edge of the Red Hen's wing. Then fill in the area with rows, following the direction of the arrows and changing colors as desired. (See "Hooking the Rug" on pages 69–70.) Following the contours of the wing gives the hen a more three-dimensional quality.

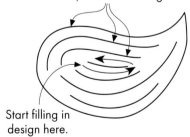

Outline first, then work design lines.

Start filling in design here.

4. Hook the center of the eye by pulling up one end of the wool in one hole and pulling up the other end in the next hole. Leave the ends of

the wool long for a moment while you hook the circle around the eye's center.

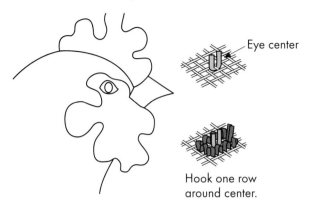

Eye center

Hook one row around center.

5. Hook the beak. Hook one row of background around its edge. Hook the brown area around the eye, the comb, the part that I unscientifically call the gobble-gobble part of the head, and the head feathers. Now you can clip the eye center's tail ends even with the tops of the wool loops (and clip any other strip ends enclosed by stitches).

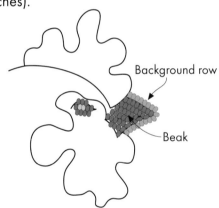

Background row

Beak

6. Continue hooking, outlining design areas and filling them in. Refer to the color key on the pullout pattern and the color photo on page 56.
7. **HENHOUSE:** Using straight-line hooking and following the lines of the siding on the henhouse pattern, hook in straight, horizontal rows. I hooked 2 rows of bright blue, 1 row of dark blue, 2 rows of bright, and 1 of dark, continuing from the top to the bottom. Depending upon your hooking style, the lines of wool loops may or may not match up with the drawn lines. (Mine did not!) But the end effect is all that matters.

8. **BACKGROUND:** I like to use many shades of one color when I hook the background areas. I pick up the colors randomly from my basket and follow the contours of the design, filling in around it. Wavy directional hooking is more interesting to look at even if you use just one solid color for your background.

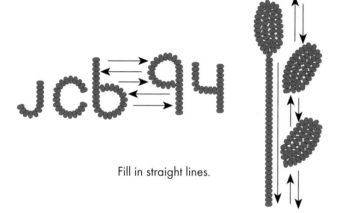

Hook in wavy lines.

9. **BORDER:** With a permanent marker, write your initials and the year somewhere in the border. Hook the letters and numbers and the grains of wheat, then, using straight lines, fill in around them with your border color. Hook a section of the border, then match the rows for the next section.

Fill in straight lines.

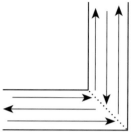

Tip

I usually draw a little diagonal line at the corners and use those lines as a guide for changing direction.

Change direction at the dotted line.

RUG CARE

♥ Roll rugs with the right side out. Never fold.
♥ Store rugs with lavender soap or sachets to prevent bug damage and to keep the rugs fresh and sweet.
♥ Gently spot clean as needed. If you must use a vacuum cleaner to clean a rug, choose a type without beaters and spinning brushes!
♥ Place a nonslip rug underlay under the rug for safety. Cut it slightly smaller than the finished rug size. Most department stores carry this product. There is a rug underlay for use on smooth floors and a different underlay for carpeted floors.

To finish your Red Hen Rug, see "Finishing the Rug" on page 71.

Rise and Shine

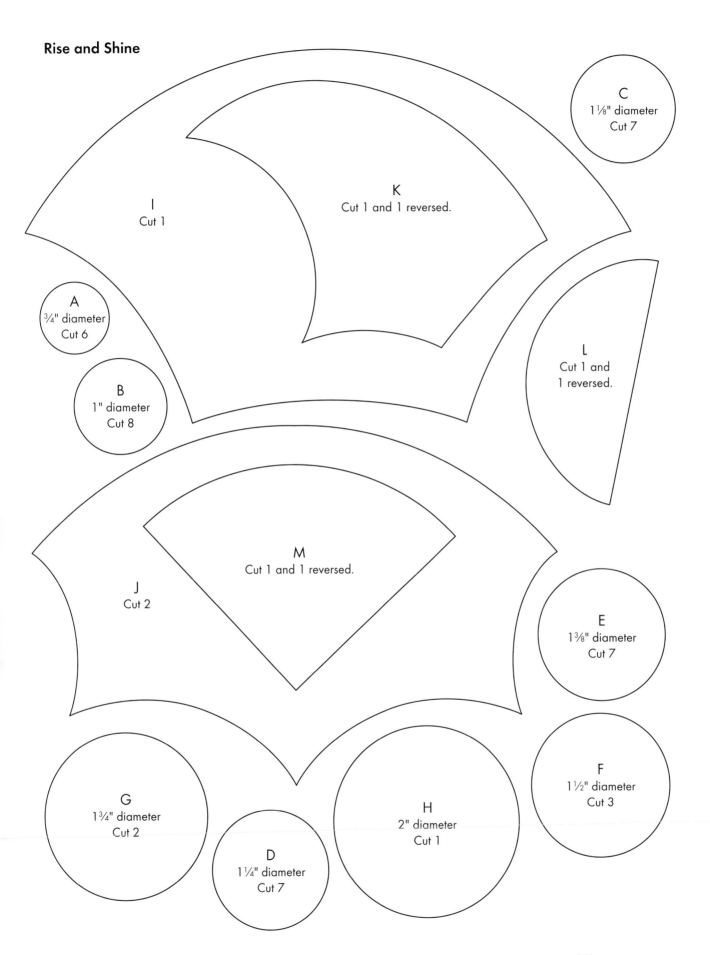

C
1 1⁄8" diameter
Cut 7

I
Cut 1

K
Cut 1 and 1 reversed.

A
3⁄4" diameter
Cut 6

B
1" diameter
Cut 8

L
Cut 1 and
1 reversed.

J
Cut 2

M
Cut 1 and 1 reversed.

E
1 3⁄8" diameter
Cut 7

F
1 1⁄2" diameter
Cut 3

G
1 3⁄4" diameter
Cut 2

D
1 1⁄4" diameter
Cut 7

H
2" diameter
Cut 1

Rise and Shine

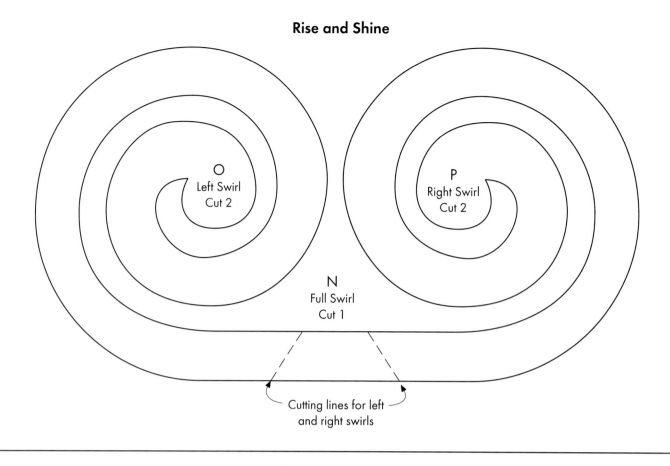

O
Left Swirl
Cut 2

P
Right Swirl
Cut 2

N
Full Swirl
Cut 1

Cutting lines for left
and right swirls

Flowers and Hearts

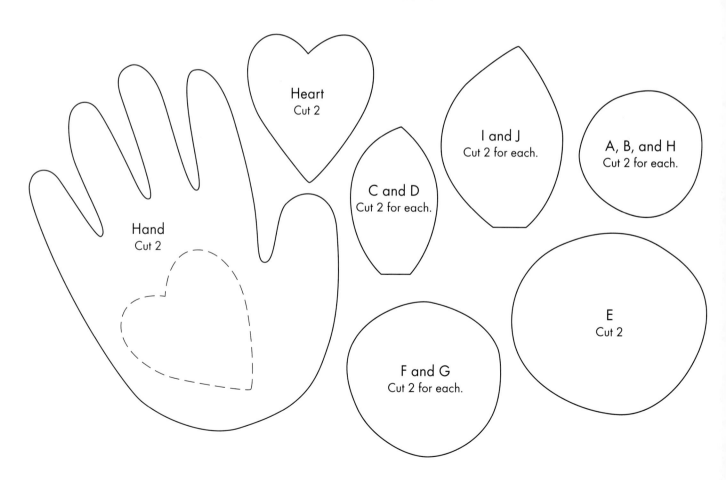

Heart
Cut 2

Hand
Cut 2

C and D
Cut 2 for each.

I and J
Cut 2 for each.

A, B, and H
Cut 2 for each.

E
Cut 2

F and G
Cut 2 for each.

40 days &
40 nights

Add Noah and windows with satin-stitch embroidery.

Cut ark from one solid piece of fabric or from several different colors.

Lion
Cut 1 and 1 reversed.

Rhinoceros
Cut 1 and 1 reversed.

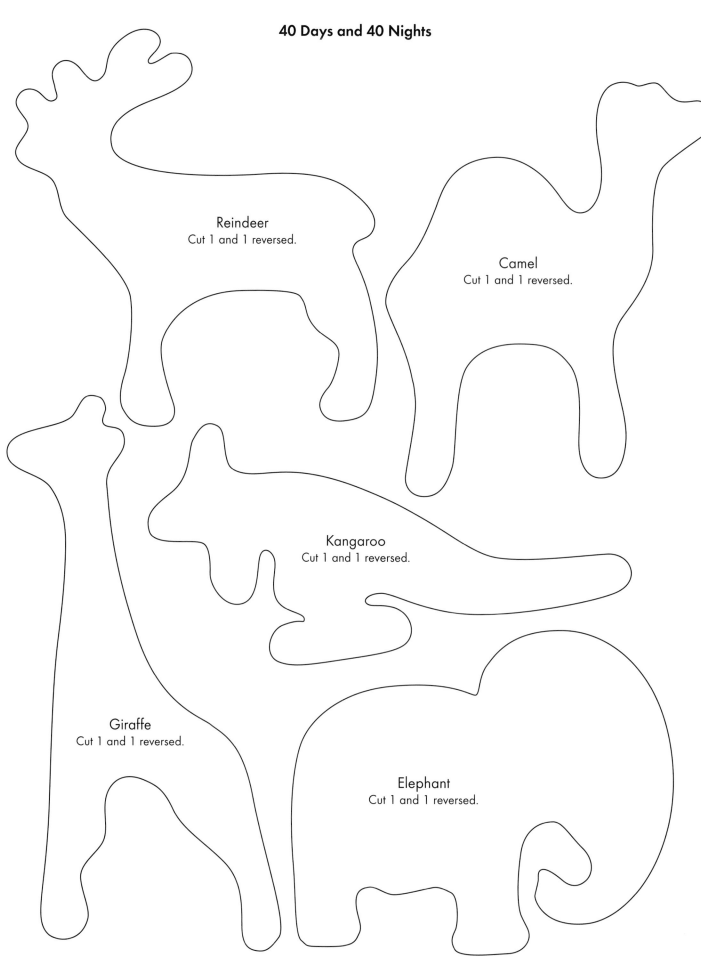

Reindeer
Cut 1 and 1 reversed.

Camel
Cut 1 and 1 reversed.

Kangaroo
Cut 1 and 1 reversed.

Giraffe
Cut 1 and 1 reversed.

Elephant
Cut 1 and 1 reversed.

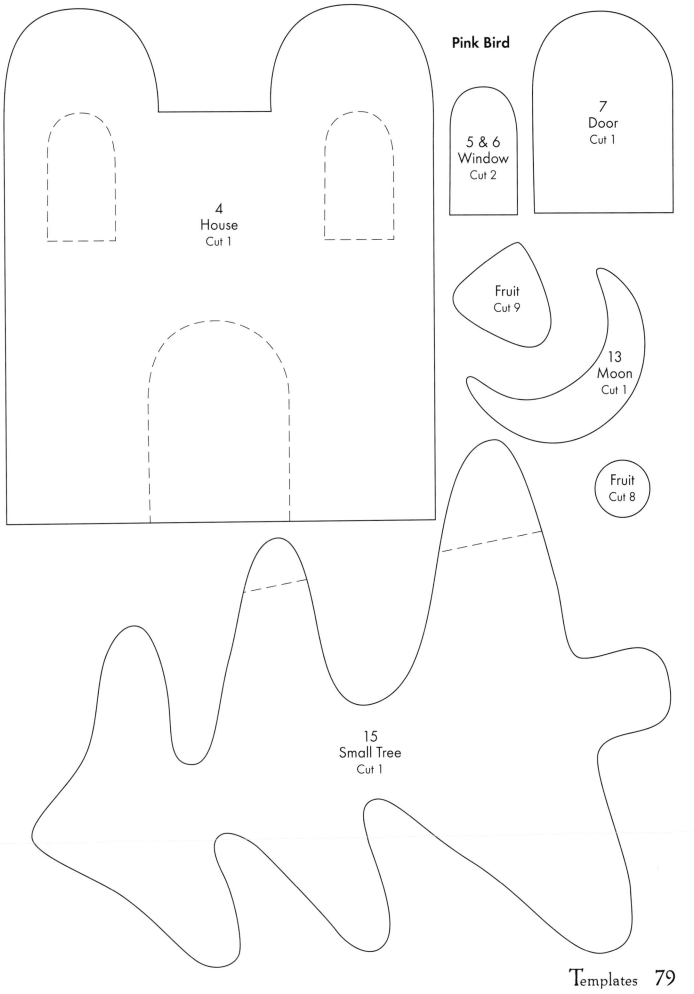

Pink Bird

5 & 6
Window
Cut 2

7
Door
Cut 1

4
House
Cut 1

Fruit
Cut 9

13
Moon
Cut 1

Fruit
Cut 8

15
Small Tree
Cut 1

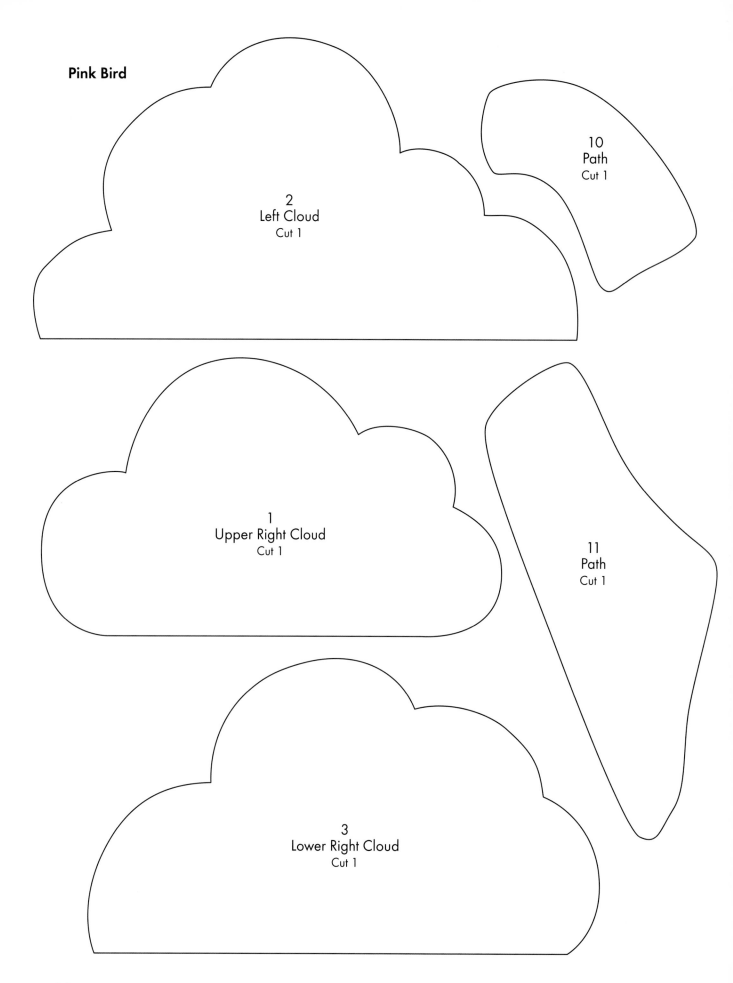

Pink Bird

2
Left Cloud
Cut 1

10
Path
Cut 1

1
Upper Right Cloud
Cut 1

11
Path
Cut 1

3
Lower Right Cloud
Cut 1

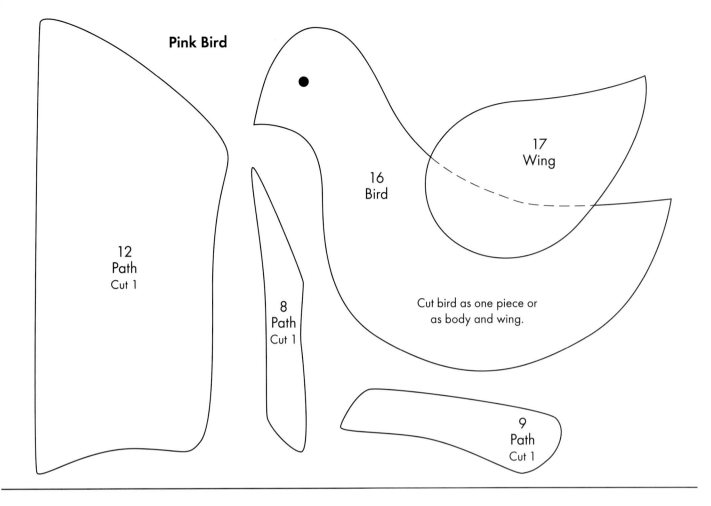

Pink Bird

12
Path
Cut 1

8
Path
Cut 1

16
Bird

17
Wing

Cut bird as one piece or
as body and wing.

9
Path
Cut 1

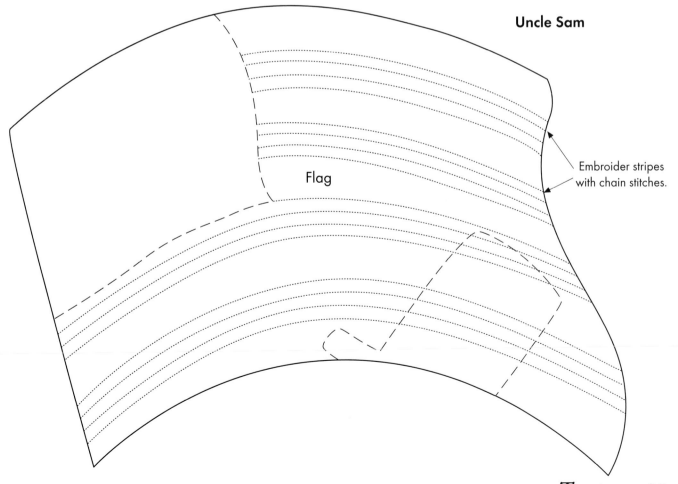

Uncle Sam

Flag

Embroider stripes
with chain stitches.

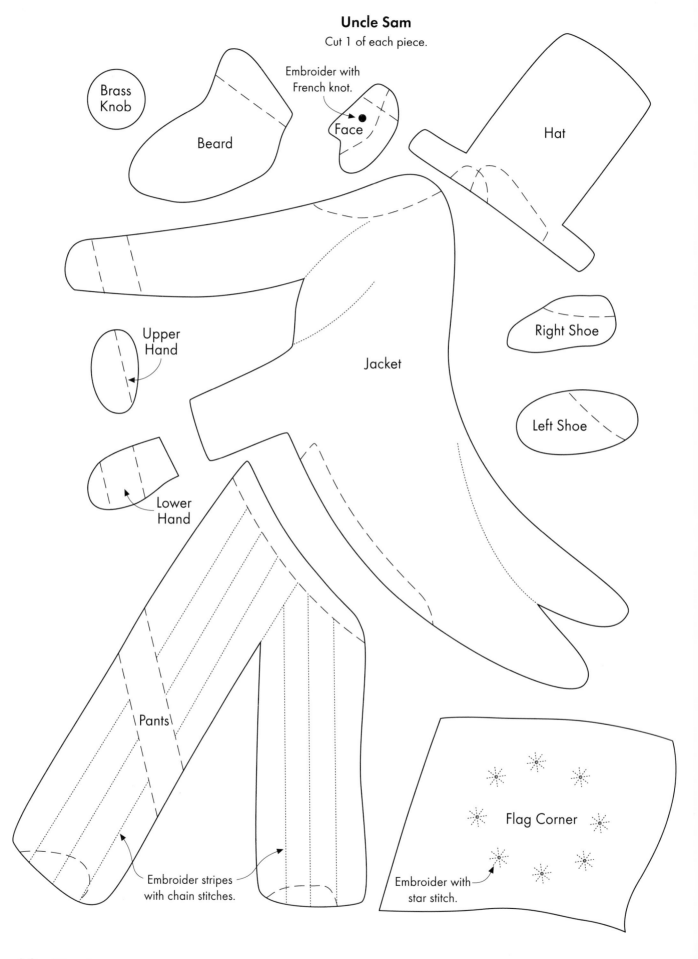

Uncle Sam
Cut 1 of each piece.

Brass Knob

Beard

Embroider with French knot.

Face

Hat

Upper Hand

Right Shoe

Jacket

Left Shoe

Lower Hand

Pants

Embroider stripes with chain stitches.

Flag Corner

Embroider with star stitch.

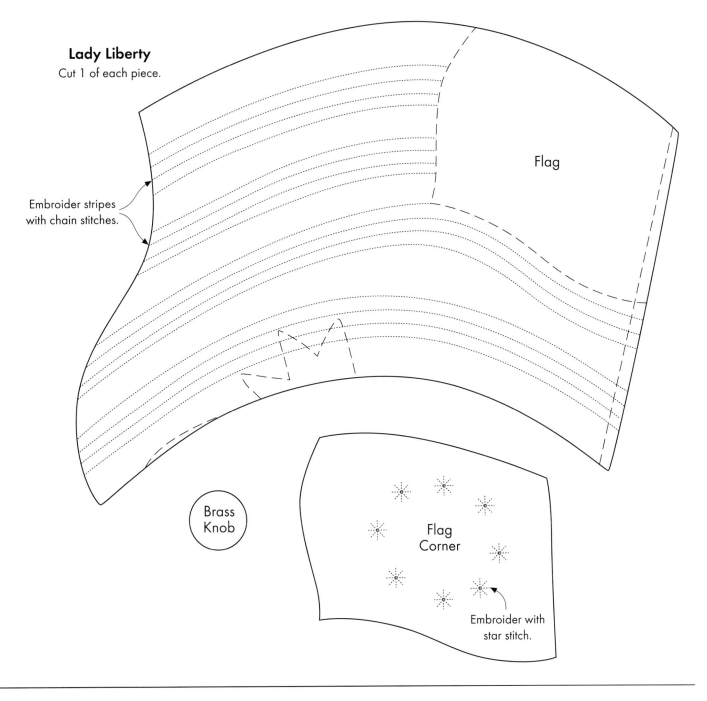

Lady Liberty
Cut 1 of each piece.

Embroider stripes
with chain stitches.

Flag

Brass
Knob

Flag
Corner

Embroider with
star stitch.

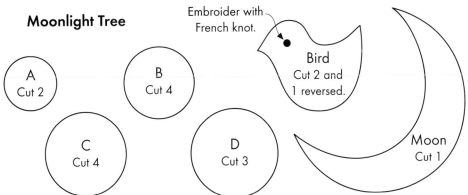

Moonlight Tree

Embroider with
French knot.

A
Cut 2

B
Cut 4

Bird
Cut 2 and
1 reversed.

C
Cut 4

D
Cut 3

Moon
Cut 1

Lady Liberty

Cut 1 of each piece.

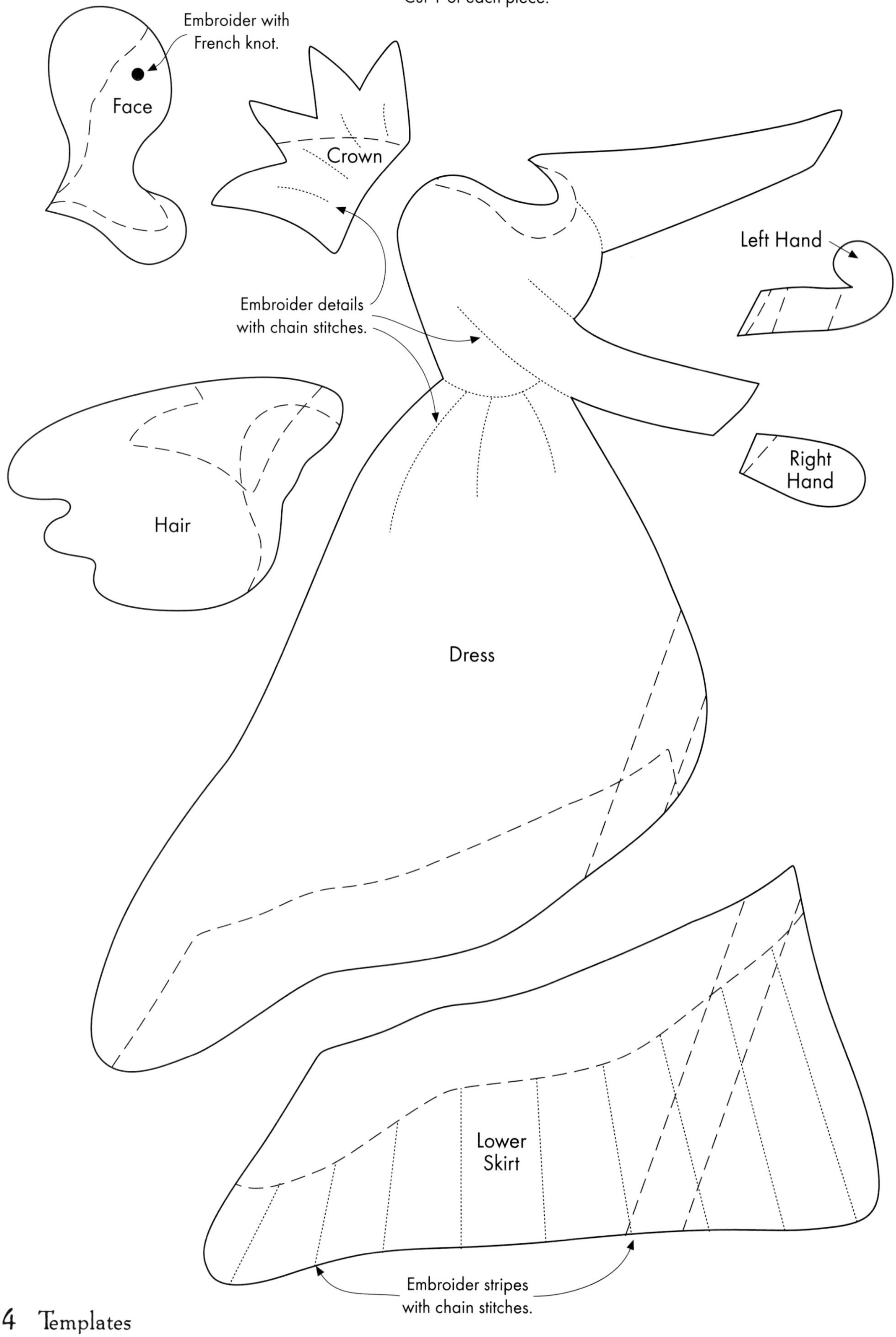

Embroider with French knot.

Face

Crown

Left Hand

Embroider details with chain stitches.

Right Hand

Hair

Dress

Lower Skirt

Embroider stripes with chain stitches.

Floral Sampler

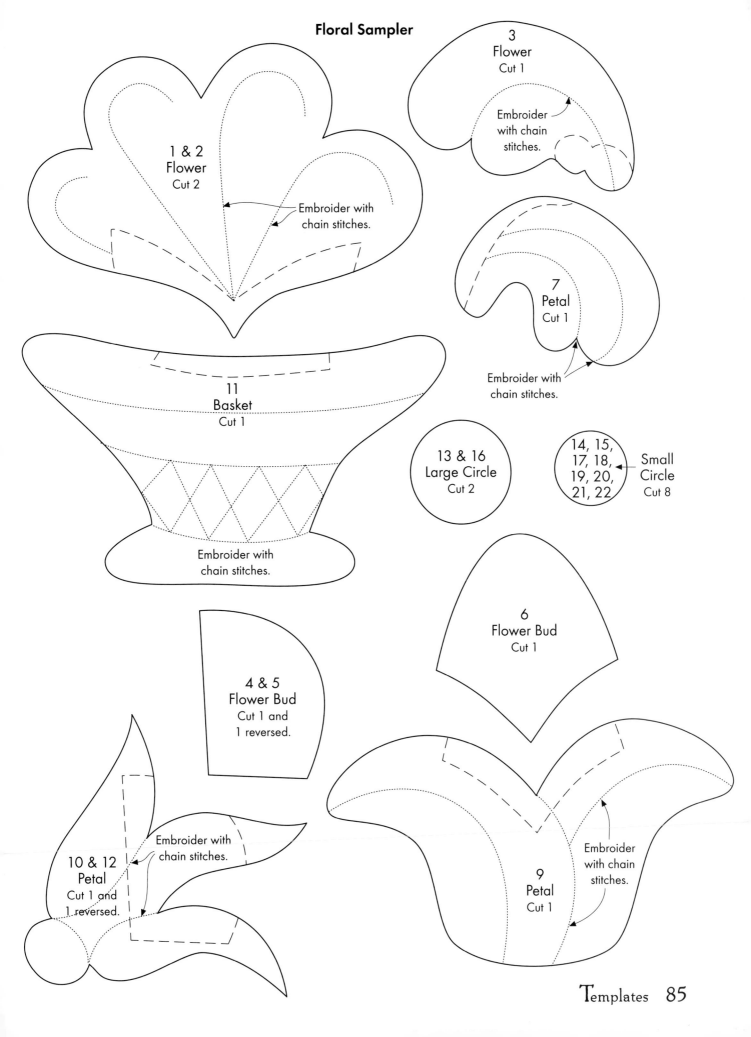

3
Flower
Cut 1

Embroider
with chain
stitches.

1 & 2
Flower
Cut 2

Embroider with
chain stitches.

7
Petal
Cut 1

Embroider with
chain stitches.

11
Basket
Cut 1

Embroider with
chain stitches.

13 & 16
Large Circle
Cut 2

14, 15,
17, 18,
19, 20,
21, 22
Small
Circle
Cut 8

6
Flower Bud
Cut 1

4 & 5
Flower Bud
Cut 1 and
1 reversed.

10 & 12
Petal
Cut 1 and
1 reversed.

Embroider with
chain stitches.

9
Petal
Cut 1

Embroider
with chain
stitches.

Templates 85

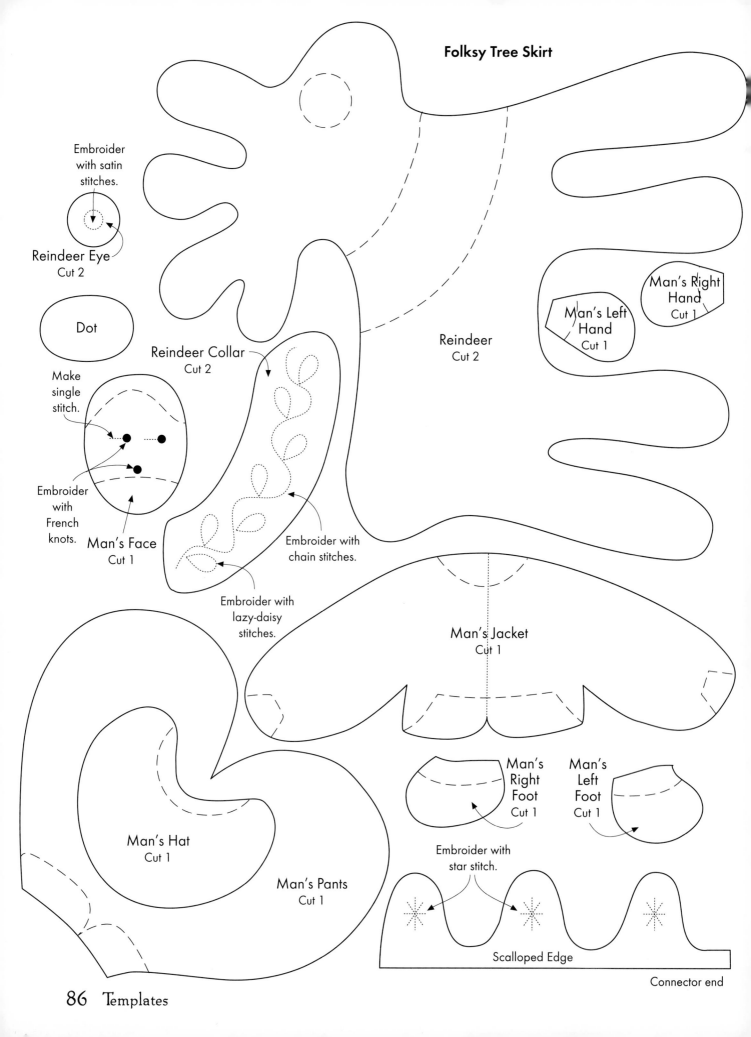

Folksy Tree Skirt

Embroider with satin stitches.

Reindeer Eye
Cut 2

Dot

Reindeer Collar
Cut 2

Reindeer
Cut 2

Man's Left
Hand
Cut 1

Man's Right
Hand
Cut 1

Make single stitch.

Embroider with French knots.

Man's Face
Cut 1

Embroider with chain stitches.

Embroider with lazy-daisy stitches.

Man's Jacket
Cut 1

Man's Hat
Cut 1

Man's Pants
Cut 1

Man's Right Foot
Cut 1

Man's Left Foot
Cut 1

Embroider with star stitch.

Scalloped Edge

Connector end

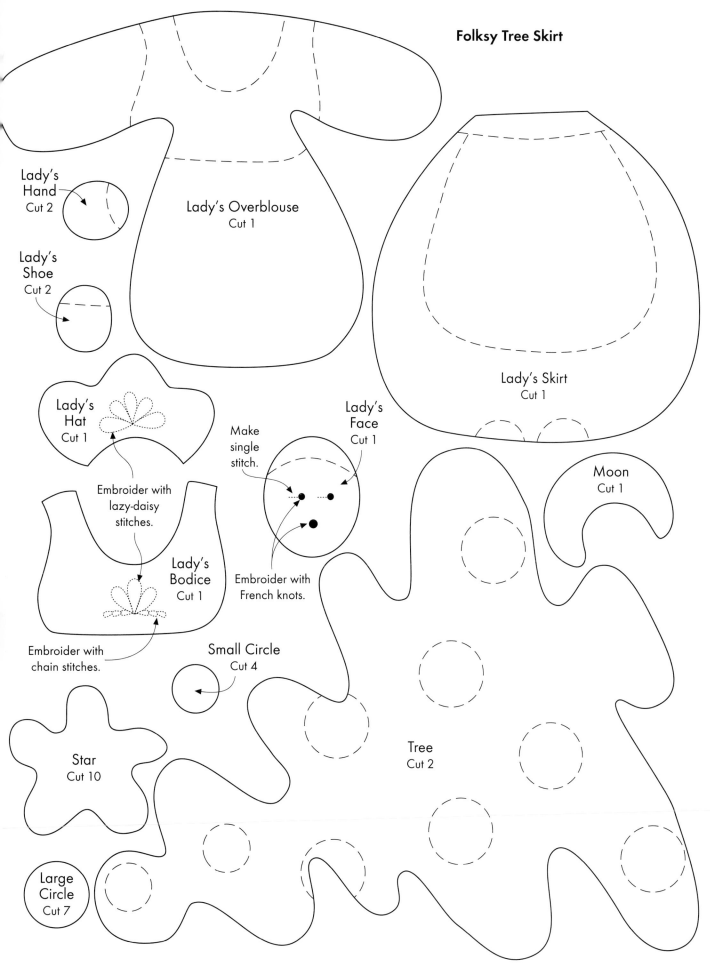

Folksy Tree Skirt

Lady's Hand
Cut 2

Lady's Overblouse
Cut 1

Lady's Skirt
Cut 1

Lady's Shoe
Cut 2

Lady's Hat
Cut 1

Make single stitch.

Lady's Face
Cut 1

Moon
Cut 1

Embroider with lazy-daisy stitches.

Lady's Bodice
Cut 1

Embroider with French knots.

Embroider with chain stitches.

Small Circle
Cut 4

Tree
Cut 2

Star
Cut 10

Large Circle
Cut 7

Resources and Inspirations

Wool and Rug Hooking Supplies
W. Cushing and Company
PO Box 351
Kennebunkport, ME 04046-0351
1-800-626-7847

Wool
B. Black & Sons—Kings Road Imports
548 South Los Angeles Street
Los Angeles CA 90013
1-800-433-1546

The Dorr Mill Store
PO Box 88
Guild, NH 03754-0088
1-800-846-DORR (3677)

Look for rug-braiding shops in your area. They usually carry a beautiful selection of heavier-weight wools.

TOD Spoon
Janet Matthews
187 Jane Drive
Syracuse, NY 13219
(315) 468-2616

Rug Hooking Frame
Appleton Krafts and Supplies
50 Appleton Avenue
So. Hamilton, MA 01982

Puritan Frame
Mayflower Textile
PO Box 329
Franklin, MA 02038-0329

Cutters
Harry M. Fraser Co.
R&R Machine Co., Inc.
433 Duggins Road
Stoneville NC 27048

Journal
Rug Hooking Magazine
PO Box 15760
Harrisburg, PA 17105-9834

Organization
Association of Traditional Hooking Artists
1360 Newman Avenue
Seekonk, MA 02771
Write for complimentary issue of bimonthly newsletter.

Suggested Reading

Moshimer, Joan. *The Complete Rug Hooker: A Guide to the Craft.* New York: Dover Books, 1975.

Bossert, Helmuth T. *Folk Art of Europe.* New York: Rizzoli Books, 1990.

Ribaric, Dr. Jelka Radaus and Szenczi, Blazena. *Yugoslavian/Croatian Folk Embroidery: Designs and Techniques.* New York: Van Nostrand Reinhold Company, 1976.

Paine, Sheila. *Embroidered Textiles: Traditional Patterns from Five Continents.* New York: Rizzoli Books, 1990.

Folk Art. Alexandria, Va: Time-Life Books, 1990.

Bond, Dorothy. *Crazy Quilt Stitches.* Self-published, 1981.